BOXING
FOR BEGINNERS

BOXING
FOR BEGINNERS

A GUIDE TO COMPETITION & FITNESS

BETTERWAY BOOKS

Cincinnati, Ohio

BILLY FINEGAN WITH **COURTNEY CLARK**
PHOTOGRAPHY BY **BRUCE CURTIS**

For more fine books from F+W Publications, visit www.fwpublications.com.

12 11 10 09 08   5 4 3 2 1

Distributed in Canada by Fraser Direct
100 Armstrong Avenue
Georgetown, Ontario, Canada L7G 5S4
Tel: (905) 877-4411

Distributed in the U.K. and Europe by David & Charles
Brunel House, Newton Abbot, Devon, TQ12 4PU, England
Tel: (+44) 1626-323200, Fax: (+44) 1626-323319
E-mail: postmaster@davidandcharles.co.uk

Distributed in Australia by Capricorn Link
P.O. Box 704, Windsor, NSW 2756 Australia
Tel: (02) 4577-3555

Library of Congress Cataloging-in-Publication Data
Finegan, Billy
  Boxing for beginners : a guide to competition and fitness / by Billy Finegan with Courtney Clark ; photographs by Bruce Curtis. -- 1st edition.
    p. cm.
  Includes index.
ISBN 978-1-55870-850-1 (pb : alk. paper)
1. Boxing. I. Title.
GV1133.F516 2008
796.83--dc22   2008019886

Edited by Michelle Ehrhard
Designed by Claudean Wheeler
Photography by Bruce Curtis
Production coordinated by Mark Griffin

F+W PUBLICATIONS, INC.

ABOUT THE AUTHORS

BILLY FINEGAN

An elite fighter on the world karate stage, Billy is also a champion in the boxing ring. As a manager and coach at Tokey Hill Martial Arts and Boxing Gym, he trains other amateur boxing athletes for national competitions. He also utilizes the boxing skills and techniques to help non-athletes at the gym enjoy the thrill of the sport while achieving full body conditioning.

- 1998–2008 Member of the U.S.A. National Karate Team

- 2008 Arnold Classic Boxing Champion

- 2007 North American Championships, Monterey, Mexico—Champion

- 2007 U.S.A. NKF Athlete of the Year

- 1998–2006 U.S.A. NKF National Karate Champion

- 2006 5th World University Karate Championship, Brooklyn, NY—World Champion

- 2006 U.S.A. Open, Las Vegas, Nevada—Bronze medal

- 2004 Pan American Karate Championship, Puerto Rico—Silver medal

- 2003 Pan American Karate Championship, Dominican Republic—Gold medal

- 2003 U.S.A. Open, Las Vegas, Nevada—Champion

- 2001 New York Daily News Golden Gloves Boxing; 178 lb. class—Champion

- 2001 World Games, Akita Japan—Silver medal

- 2000 2nd World University Karate Championship, Yokohama, Japan—Bronze medal

COURTNEY CLARK

Courtney is a longtime sports enthusiast. She was captain of her high school cheerleading squad and also played varsity volleyball and golf. She has ghost written three books on golf and is currently writing a how-to book on baseball.

She is a fitness instructor at Tokey Hill World Champion Karate in Roslyn, New York, and leads fitness seminars.

PHOTOGRAPHER BRUCE CURTIS

Bruce has chronicled many of the significant events of the last decades of the twentieth century as a photographer for *Time*, *LIFE*, and *Sports Illustrated*. He has been on the front lines of the Vietnam War, covered the explorations of Jacques Cousteau, and captured the glory of the Papal Archives and the action on the fast-paced sports field.

His uncanny ability to capture the significant moment led Bruce to explore special effects with MIT physicist and Nobel Laureate, Dr. Harold Edgerton. His interest in action photography inspired Bruce to use pyrotechnics and laser light to create the "action still life," a combination of the best of special effects and still life photography in one dynamic image. The demand for his images in posters, calendars, books, greeting cards, and CD ROMs continues to grow.

ACKNOWLEDGMENTS

There are many people who have helped us in the creation of this book:

- Billy thanks the two biggest inspirations in his life: his coach, Tokey Hill, and his dad, Joseph Finegan. It has been rewarding to always have them in his corner.

- Courtney thanks her boys, Ian and Zachery, for their love and support.

- Special thanks to Tony Garcia, Billy's trainer, who gave valuable advice throughout the book. We wish continued success to his company Fitness Pros in Great Neck, New York (www.thefitnesspros.net).

- We would not have been able to make this book happen without the invaluable knowledge, assistance, and support of Christina Muccini and Kassiem Elliott.

- And for helping with pictures and general support, a thank you to Ashley Hill, Annemarie DeVivo, and Joni Spencer.

TABLE OF CONTENTS

VII. BAG WORK

VIII. CONDITIONING

IX. COOL DOWN

X. THE ULTIMATE BOXING WORKOUT

XI. GETTING INTO THE RING

FOREWORD

Boxing is a great sport because after you have trained yourself to the limit, you get to put that training to the test in a one to one contest that puts it all on the line. I should know; there is nothing as beautiful as the adrenaline rush of winning the World Heavyweight Championship, especially as the underdog. Training and conditioning gave me the edge against Mike Tyson in our 1990 championship bout in Tokyo, Japan. I knocked him out in the 10th round, but to be able to go the rounds of a professional match takes a lot of stamina, endurance, and strength. Boxing training is designed specifically to give you those things.

After I won the championship, I put on some weight, which led to health problems that eventually resulted in a diabetic coma. I knew that I had to get back into shape or pay the ultimate price. I returned to the gym and started boxing again. Not only did I lose 117 pounds, but I was able to stage a comeback in the ring where I won the next eight out of nine fights before retiring for good.

Boxing training works, and you don't need to have dreams of a title to make it work for you. This book, *Boxing for Beginners: A Guide to Competition and Fitness*, can help to prepare you for the fight of your life, or it can simply help you get into the best shape of your life. Take it from me—it's a knockout.

—BUSTER DOUGLAS, world heavyweight
boxing champion, 1990

CHAPTER ONE

GETTING STARTED

Boxing has been around for centuries, so if you are looking for the latest fad workout, keep right on looking. If you are looking for a total body cardio workout that you can do in your own home or apartment, keep reading. If you are interested in the competitive aspects of the sport, this book will teach you essential boxing skills in a step-by-step fashion. I'll guide you in beginner sparring as well as how to put it all together to take it to a higher level: amateur competition.

I have been boxing since I was nine years old and have won numerous amateur competitions, including the New York Daily News Golden Gloves in 2001. As a member of the U.S. Olympic Team for karate since 1998, I have had access to the best and latest in training and conditioning. In addition to my own competitive schedule, I train and coach many amateur boxers for competition. I also train my co-author, Courtney, who like many of my clients enjoys boxing training to achieve personal fitness goals and for self defense.

Boxing matches have been documented as far back as ancient Greece and Rome, where fighters would wrap their hands in leather. But the sport as we know it today, with boxing gloves and three-minute rounds, dates to 1865 when John Chambers established twelve rules for boxing under the sponsorship of the Marquess of Queensbury. The rules became known as the Marquess of Queensbury rules. The first "sanctioning body" for the sport that arranged matches and ranked fighters started in 1927. Today, boxing is a major sport in both professional and amateur levels, including in the Olympic Games.

Boxing has recently gained popularity in a whole new way: it has moved from the world of fighting to the world of fitness. Traditionally found only in hard-core training gyms in urban areas, boxing can now be found in neighborhood health centers and fitness classes. Men and women of all abilities have begun to appreciate boxing for what it can do to make the body physically fit while improving their confidence and reducing stress. Many professional people, such as doctors and lawyers, have discovered the thrill of amateur fighting in what is called white collar boxing.

BENEFITS OF BOXING

So, boxing isn't just pummeling people and learning to take a punch? Of course not. Boxing offers a complex workout that builds endurance, stamina, and physical fitness. And it can do all this for you.

For a start, you will be using muscles in all the areas of your body. In the upper body, boxers strengthen the trapezius muscle at the back of the neck, the deltoid muscle over the shoulder, biceps and triceps on the front and back of the arms, and the pectoral or chest muscles. The lower body muscles that are important for boxing include the gluteus maximus or rump muscle, the quadriceps femoris and hamstrings at the front and back of the thighs, and the calf muscles. Especially important is a boxer's core made up of the abdominal muscles, called the rectus abdominis, and the latissimus dorsi, the muscle that covers the middle and lower back area over your kidneys. Although you will be doing some weight resistance exercises, and the weight of the gloves definitely adds to the workout, there is no actual weight lifting. As a result, your muscles will be strong, toned, and well defined without looking bulky.

You'll be amazed at how punching can tighten up the abs and strengthen the back, giving you better posture. You'll feel good and stand tall. Just as the act of smiling will actually improve your mood, feeling more confident can actually make you more confident. Punching the bag can also be a great surrogate for dealing with other things you'd like to punch. Visualize the stressful things in your life as the bag, and get some of the unproductive emotions out of your system.

EQUIPMENT

So, what do you need to get started? You should be fully equipped and ready to go for under $200. All the items you need are available at any sporting goods store or sporting supply catalogs, such as Everlast or Ringside, or online. Here is a shopping list for the equipment to get you started:

- heavy bag
- speed bag
- double end bag
- jump rope
- medicine ball
- timer
- gloves and wraps

Let's start with the main attraction: *bags*! You can't learn to land a punch unless you have something to punch. There are three types of bags that we'll be using in the workout: the heavy bag, the speed bag, and the double end bag. These are the mainstays of the competitive boxer's essential training as well. In chapter seven we will learn how to use them.

Heavy Bag

This is your biggest piece of equipment, and as the name implies, it's *heavy*. We suggest a 60-pound bag as a good all-around weight to use, but you need to have a beam in your house, garage, or apartment that can handle it. You will find heavy bags in synthetic leathers for light to moderate use at about seventy dollars that are excellent for a beginner, and real leather or canvas for heavy-duty use. Most bags are filled with sand, which can make transporting them a problem if you have to carry a heavy one any distance or up or down a flight of stairs. Another option is a water

1.1 HEAVY BAG

heavy bag, which is easy to transport. The water bag—purchased empty—runs about $120. It can then be filled with water at home up to about 80 pounds. The bag can be made harder or softer depending on how much you fill it. It gives a great resistance and has the most similar feel to actually landing a punch on an opponent.

If you don't have the right support to hang a heavy bag, you have a few other options:

- **Get a bag stand.** This is a freestanding hanging frame that can often hold a speed bag, as well as a double end bag. The stand takes up more room but it can fit in a corner pretty easily. The frame itself is not as durable as hanging the bag on a beam in the garage or basement but it is fine for getting started.

- **Get a Wavemaster or a freestanding heavy bag.** This is a water-filled plastic stand with a bag that slides onto a post on top. It is durable but does take up some space. Although it can be rolled around the room, once you've got it filled with water, it is pretty much staying wherever you put it because of its weight.

- **Get an air bag.** This bag hangs the same way the heavy bag does but is also attached to a weight at the bottom to give more resistance. You just fill it with a bicycle pump-type inflator. Although it does not give the heavy resistance that a sand- or water-filled bag does, it works pretty well and is ideal for multipurpose areas, as it is lightweight and easily unhooks and deflates to move or store flat in a closet.

Speed Bag

You know this one—it's the bag they feature in all the movies that is tethered to the ceiling. Whether it's Hilary Swank taking it slow and deliberate in *Million Dollar Baby* or Sylvester Stallone getting with the triple rhythm

in any *Rocky* movie, this is the one that looks like so much fun. And it is! This bag will help you learn speed, timing, rhythm, and accuracy. It is ideal for building muscle endurance in your shoulders. When choosing a speed bag for your boxing workout, there are only a few options. The key is that for a beginner, bigger is better because speed bags can be tricky to hit and you have a better chance at making contact when learning with a larger bag. For starting out, you can get a bag complete with hanging platform and swivel hook for hanging the bag, starting at about sixty dollars. You will need the platform above the bag because the bag will bounce off the platform when you hit it. If you already have access to a platform, a vinyl bag sized about 11" x 8" or 10" x 7" for around thirty dollars is a good pick. Just be sure that when you hang it, the fattest part of the bag is by your nose and mouth. If it's too high or too low, you won't be using the proper punching techniques and won't be getting the most out of your workout.

Double End Bag

Like the speed bag, this bag also helps develop speed, timing, and quick reflexes. It is tethered to the floor as well as the ceiling, hence the name double end, with a tough rubber cord that snaps back or rebounds very quickly. They come in 6", 7", and 9" sizes. As a beginner, the larger 9" bag (for around forty dollars) is going to be easier to learn with simply because there is more surface area to try to hit. The bottom is usually anchored with a sand bag weighted to about 35 pounds.

Part of the beauty of boxing training is that the accessories are basic. Here are some other things you will need:

Jump Rope

Although it may seem too basic, a jump rope is a great piece of equipment—and you won't need nursery rhymes! Check out any serious gym and you'll find an array of ropes to choose from. They are great for cardio, speed, and agility work.

If you are new to jumping, you may want to start with a beaded rope. These are a little slower and will let you develop your rhythm more easily.

A speed rope is usually made of leather or plastic and is a better choice once you've gotten the hang of jumping rope because it helps in develop-

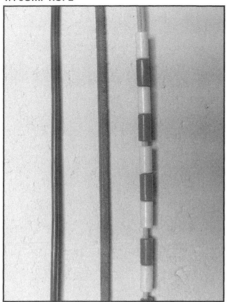 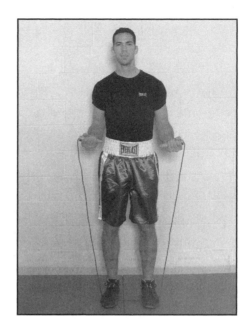

ing your footwork. Fortunately, ropes cost about ten dollars or less, so it is not a big investment to buy a speed rope later on.

The length of the rope is the most important thing. Measure it by standing in the middle of the rope and holding the handles up. They should reach to chest level just under the armpits. You can always modify the length by snipping off a few inches or tying a knot, but be careful not to go too short or you'll not be able to move as freely.

Medicine Ball

These balls come in a range of weights from about 5 to 50 pounds. Although a good overall weight is 10 pounds, the correct weight will vary depending on your size and strength. To find out what is a good weight for you, do some reps in the store, standing with your legs hip distance apart and holding the ball at chest height. Extend your arms fully in front of you, being sure to keep your elbows slightly bent on the extension so that you do not overextend, and

then back into your chest about thirty times. Your arms should feel fatigued but you should be able to do it. If you don't feel fatigued, go heavier. If you are not able to do thirty reps while maintaining posture, go lighter.

Medicine balls may be made of leather or rubber and may be hard or filled with sand. We recommend the hard rubber ones because they will be useful during the solo workout. You'll be able to bounce the ball off the floor or the wall for great resistance training.

Timer

Get a three-minute timer. Boxing for the ring or a workout is built on three-minute intervals followed by one minute of rest. You can get all the bells and whistles (not to mention flashing lights) on a hundred-dollar-plus boxing timer if you want super motivation, but any simple timer with a buzzer will do. An inexpensive and convenient option is a timer on a Velcro band that you can affix around your upper arm. We do recommend getting a timer with a buzzer rather than using a basic egg timer or

simply watching a clock, because, when you are working out, you'll want to put all of your focus on your punches, not on checking out the time. A timer will also regulate the breaks between sets of exercises or rounds that are integral to a boxer's training.

And finally, we get to your gear. You'll need gloves and wraps, whatever workout apparel you are comfortable in, and any pair of cross-training shoes with good support. Boxing shoes, available in sporting goods stores, are not essential when you start out, but you will want them as you get more involved with the sport. Cross-trainers are fine for your beginning workouts, and they are necessary for the running portions of your training because boxing shoes do not offer enough support.

Gloves

Gloves come in different weights. The lighter 8-ounce gloves are for ring fighting, where you want the least weight resistance to avoid fatigue and little padding to insure maximum force with each punch.

For training you want gloves with some heft to them—between 14 and 18 ounces—so that the resistance adds to the workout. For beginners, an additional benefit to the heavier gloves is that they are more padded. Although a boxing workout stresses speed and technique over hitting hard, a well-padded glove will make you more comfortable as you learn and will make you less likely to end up with bruised knuckles.

In addition, I recommend getting gloves with the Velcro or hoop-and-loop closure instead of the lace-ups, because putting the lace-ups on can be a two-person job. If you'll be doing the workout alone, using hoop-and-loop closure gloves will allow you to get your gloves on by yourself much easier and faster.

Wraps

Wraps are padding around the wrists and hands that are worn under the boxing gloves. They protect and add support in much the same way a bandage supports a sprain. Whether or not to use them is a personal choice. However, I strongly recommend using them. First, your hands have a lot of small bones, and it makes sense to protect them. After all, an injury is going to slow you down and keep you from your workout and competition. Second, wraps add padding and will make punching more comfortable so you can focus on your technique.

There is not much selection when it comes to buying a wrap, and they range in price from less than two to five dollars. A wrap looks like a bandage with a thumb loop to hold it in place. They are usually made of cotton, which will absorb sweat and make wearing the gloves more comfortable. They can easily be thrown in the wash as well, so an added benefit is that they save the gloves from getting too smelly.

A more expensive, but vastly more convenient, alternative to the traditional bandage-style wrap is a glove wrap. These run about twenty dollars and are great for beginners because, instead of taking five minutes at the start of your workout just to get your wraps on, you can slip on the gloves in a couple of seconds. The gloves have some gel padding over the knuckles so you can also wear them alone for light bag work.

HANDS AND GLOVES

Now that you know what equipment you'll need, let's learn the very basics about how to get your hands ready. Start with wrapping your hands since that is what you'll need to do before you can start doing any punches. Once you get your hands wrapped, we'll learn how to get your hands positioned properly in your gloves so that you can begin trying the fun stuff. It takes a couple of minutes to put the wrap on, but the added comfort and protection are worth it. There are a few different ways to wrap your hands, but this is the basic way that I show the people I train.

Wrapping Your Hands

STEP 1: Hold your hand out flat with fingers spread apart. Place the thumb loop over the thumb making sure that the "This Side Down" writing is against your skin. (If your wrap does not have this text, mark the skin side with a pen for future reference. This will ensure that the Velcro is on the correct side for fastening and save lots of re-wrapping down the road.) Wrap around the back of your hand and around your wrist two or three

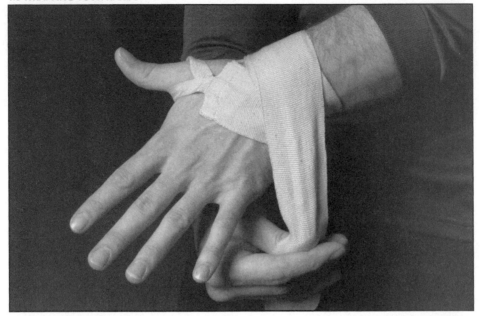

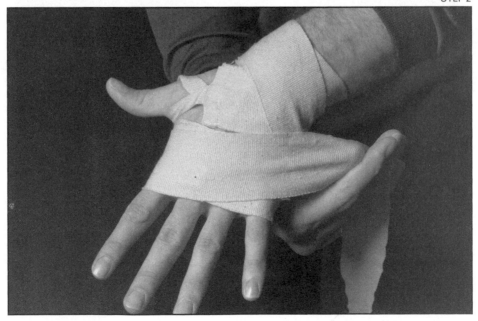

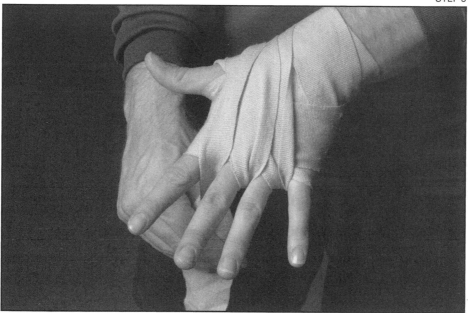

times so that the area about two inches above your wrist is supported. Circulation is a good thing, so the key is to make it snug but not tight.

STEP 2: Now, bring the wrap from the wrist up the back of the hand to the baseline of your fingers, cross over your palm and then over the tops of your knuckles. Repeat this two or three times, making an X pattern on the back of your hand.

STEP 3: This step is all about the thumb and fingers. First, wrap the base and around the thumb. Then wrap back around the hand and around the thumb in the other direction. Don't twist the wrap—always keep it flat.

Now, take the wrap from just below your thumb and across your hand in between the little finger and the ring finger. Then move it down across your palm and back up under your thumb to wrap between the ring finger and middle finger. Repeat this process between the middle and index fingers.

Now that all fingers have been separated, wrap over the knuckles once more.

STEP 4: Finally, wrap down toward your wrist and secure the wrap with either the hook and loop or the Velcro. Repeat the same process to wrap your other hand.

STEP 5: Practice making a fist to make sure that you get the proper positioning of the hand and wrist. Using a mirror will be helpful.

Getting on Your Gloves

Now that your hands are ready to go, let's make sure you get them in the proper position in the glove.

STEP 1: Curl your fingers down so that your fingertips touch your palm.

STEP 2: Curl your thumb on the *outside* of your fingers so that the thumbnail rests between the knuckles of your index and middle fingers. Remember that a thumb *inside* the curled fingers means a broken thumb. Your hands should be relaxed and there should be a straight line down your arm. It is very important that your wrist not

1.8 WRAPPING YOUR HANDS   STEP 4

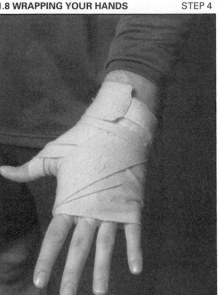

STEP 5

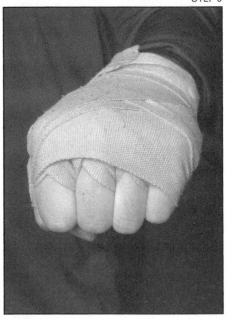

bend up or down but that it maintain an unbroken line with your forearm. The knuckles of your index and middle fingers should be leading.

STEP 3: Now we are ready to slip on the glove. As you put the glove on, you will feel that it is constructed to hold your hand in the lightly fisted position. Tighten the strap to where it feels secure yet comfortable. Do not make it overly tight; you do not want to constrict your muscles during the workout.

CHAPTER TWO

STANCE

Even though you might want to begin with punching, it's important to first learn a proper stance. You may have been standing your whole life, but you need to make yourself aware of your foot positioning, your weight distribution, and your overall body posture to achieve the necessary balance and leverage to move efficiently and effectively. A proper fighter's stance is the key element to swift multi-directional movement with the balance that allows you to fire punches in attack mode and to evade your opponent's blows in defense mode.

HOW TO STAND

If you are right-handed, you will stand with your left foot forward (figure 2.1 on page 20). Your dominant hand will always be your power punching hand. You want that side of your body to be furthest away from the bag or your opponent because as you lean forward to punch you throw your body weight behind it for maximum impact. If you are left-handed, what boxers call "southpaw," stand with your right foot forward.

Practice stance and movement in front of a full-length mirror until it feels like second nature. In chapter five, we will discuss shadow boxing, and the mirror will be essential to that part of the workout.

To practice your stance, first stand with your legs shoulder-width apart, with your left foot in front of your right foot if you are right-handed (figure 2.2 on page 21). If you are left-handed, do the opposite for all of the instructions. Do not point your feet straight ahead (at your opponent) but at a 45-degree angle so that your whole body is angled toward your opponent. This angle creates the ability to move around the ring easily while at the same time presenting a smaller target area for your opponent to hit.

Keep your knees slightly bent. Bending the knees creates the ability to balance and allows swift, dynamic movement, whether forward and backward, side-to-side, or to a downward crouch in order to duck a punch.

Distribute your weight equally between your front and back legs. Lift your heels *slightly* and put the weight on the balls of your feet.

Hold your elbows close to your body, lightly touching your ribs (figure 2.3). Hold your hands in front of your chin with your palms facing each other. Make light to moderately tight fists—not tense, tight fists.

Keep your stomach tight and your shoulders slightly hunched in a crouched position.

For protection, tuck your chin slightly into your left shoulder.

Now that you've gotten the basic position, *relax*—and stay relaxed!

Speed and agility are not all about muscle movement. The neurological process that sends messages from the brain to your muscles functions better through open pathways. Tense, tight muscles block those pathways, which will make you move and respond more slowly and tire more quickly. Think:

- Tension = Fatigue and decreased stamina
- Relaxed = Increased speed and stamina

2.2

2.3

So take a deep breath and let it out slowly. Feel yourself relax before you start your workout. If you feel tension in your shoulders, try to breathe it out and let it go. Are your fists squeezed? Loosen them up a little so that you are not restricting your movement. Are your knees rigid, or can you bounce easily?

Although it may seem counterintuitive, you will have a more rapid response time in the ring if you are relaxed. Nervousness makes us tense, and just as we cannot control our muscles as effectively when we are tense, neither can we think as clearly or as quickly. You will be a much more effective and dynamic fighter when your reactions and response time are sharpened with clear thought.

FOOTWORK

Now for some basic rules about moving so that you don't get yourself tangled up. The general rule is that you always keep your feet in the same relative position that we just learned in the stance (figures 2.1 and 2.2).

2.4
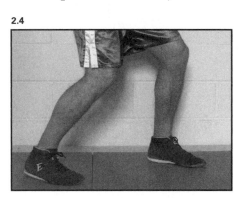

2.5
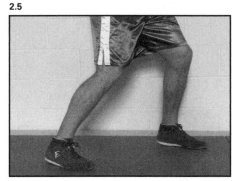

When moving forward, always step with your front foot first (figure 2.4), then follow with your back leg (figure 2.5). So, if you are right-handed, you will step forward with your left foot, then follow with the right.

Moving backward follows the same principle. Step with your back foot first (figure 2.6), and then follow with the front foot (figure 2.7).

When moving from side to side, lead with the left foot when moving left and the right foot when moving right (figures 2.8 and 2.9). Don't make any grapevine moves (crossing your right over your left or vice versa), or you will lose your balance if you are hit.

Whichever direction you are moving, be sure to keep your feet and body on a 45-degree angle toward the bag or opponent so that you are always ready to fire a punch (figure 2.10).

Practicing in front of a mirror helps to view your form. Let's review some of the common mistakes that you should watch out for.

- **Crossing your feet.** Never do this, as you will lose your balance and lose your form.

- **Being flat-footed.** This will really slow you down. Stay on your toes to stay agile and move quickly.

- **Losing proper stance.** Many people lose the proper stance once their footwork becomes faster. You need to maintain proper stance for power, leverage, and balance. If you find yourself losing the proper stance, slow it down.

- **Bouncing like a bunny.** It is a common misconception that boxers should bounce. What you are seeing when you watch a fighter is not bouncing; it is rhythm and readiness. Think and feel like a cat, light on your feet with your heels off the ground.

Now that we have the mechanics down, let's talk about the strategy behind the footwork and how to use it as a tool in your fighting. Moving forward is an aggressive stance when you are stalking or attacking your opponent. Backwards movement is primarily to evade; however, it is not just a retreat. You can still throw punches as you move back or get out of the way. You can fight moving both forwards and backwards. Lateral movements allow you to create openings to attack as well as deflection moves to avoid getting hit.

Remember, you are the *target*. It is harder to hit a moving target, so the object is to *not be stationary*. Keep moving to get out of the way.

Speed and endurance are essential here. Obviously, to keep moving in a fight you need to have a high fitness factor. Also, these movements need to become second nature so that in a fight you are concentrating your energies on what your opponent is doing and where your opportunities lie, not on where you are putting your feet. Shadow boxing and jumping rope, skills that are discussed in chapter five, will help get you to this level. Working with the bags, which is discussed in chapter seven, will also train your footwork.

CHAPTER THREE

PUNCHING

As you know, a good offense is essential to a boxer's success in the ring. Many components make up a good offense, such as the mastery of footwork in closing or widening the gap between you and your opponent that we discussed in chapter two. But your primary offensive technique will be your ability to land punches with speed, power, and precision while maintaining a strong defense. Throwing a punch will only win you the match if your defensive tactics are "on point." The ability to get in close and deliver a blow while simultaneously defending yourself will give you the advantage. In chapter four we'll talk in more detail about the importance of defense. In this chapter we will focus on instructing you in the basic offensive techniques that will give you the solid foundation needed to knock out your opponent, or as they say in the ring, bring them "to the canvas."

Punching is the meat of a boxing workout, and it is the core activity in the art of hand combat. So, in addition to being your primary offensive tactic, punching is what will tone your arms, develop your core abdominal strength, increase your endurance, and aid in weight loss. It's my favorite part of the workout because it really gets the adrenaline pumping.

Before we talk about the actual punches, let's spend a moment on the mechanics of what is happening with your muscles, specifically in your fist, when you punch. Muscles work when you tense *and* when you relax them. It takes a lot of energy to keep a muscle tense, so if you stay tense throughout a workout or a fight, your muscles are not being given a beneficial workout and will be overtired and strained. We will discuss the dynamic between muscle tension and relaxation as it pertains to the particular body area focus throughout the lessons in the book.

For punching, keep your fist relaxed in the glove; tighten it just before impact with the bag or your opponent. The fist should be tightened for only that split second of impact, and then you should relax again. This gives your punch more power and conserves your energy.

So let's get started learning about the different punches and how to do them.

The jab is one of the most important punches a fighter will learn in boxing. It is the most frequently thrown punch because it serves as a measuring tool to get close to your opponent to set up combinations. If you can hit with a jab, then you are the right distance to fire a combination of punches. In conjunction with footwork, the jab is effective in controlling your distance from your opponent. If you are too far away to hit your target with a jab and must first step toward it, then you are "on the outside." If you are so close to the target that you must take a step back to hit it with a jab, then you are "on the inside." If you can reach out and hit your target without moving, then you are "in range."

Muhammad Ali was memorable for his controlling the distance in a fight while still inflicting massive damage on his opponent. He controlled the distance and the tempo of the fight with a combination of his superior footwork and his long arms. He danced around the ring to tire his opponent out while he kept himself out of range. By virtue of his long reach, he could then step in close and deliver his punches, the vast majority of which were jabs, and dance out of range again to avoid the counterpunches. This ability to land a punch at arm's length, as opposed to a body punch, is a characteristic of a far-range punch. A far-range punch does not work as well for smaller, stockier fighters without the reach. Part of learning to fight is developing a style that works for your body type and makes the most of your natural skills, such as power, speed, agility, or endurance. We will be going into greater detail on developing personal style and recognizing an opponent's style in the sparring section in chapter eleven on page 152.

Remember that the keys to an effective jab are *speed* and *snap*. Think of Ali dancing in close, delivering a blow, and getting out—speed. The snap comes from a crisp delivery where you tense up the fist at the second of impact.

STEP 1: Start in the fighting stance with your hands up by your face, your palms facing each other, and your elbows in to your body. Keep your chin down and your eyes forward, focused on your opponent.

STEP 2: Coming straight off the chin, extend your lead fist (typically your left, if you are right-handed) toward your opponent's head with a snapping motion. Come out fast and go back fast. Make sure when you throw a jab that you keep a straight line with your arm from the shoulder, elbow, wrist, and knuckles out towards the bag and back again. Remember to turn your wrist as you extend your punch, going from palms facing each other in the guard position to palm facing down upon making impact with the front two knuckles of your index and middle fingers.

Your non-punching arm should stay in guard position in front of your body. A common mistake is to let this arm drift out to the side, which will leave you open to attack.

3.1 JAB   STEP 1

STEP 2

Let's review how the jab can work both stepping toward the bag and stepping away. If you need to close the gap and step forward, do so with your left foot first, then follow with the right (reverse if you are left-handed). Remember to keep your legs hip-width apart and diagonal to each other so you don't lose balance. If the bag is swinging toward you and you need to retreat while still punching, step back first with your right foot and then follow with your left. The step forward or backward is simultaneous to the punch itself.

RIGHT CROSS

The right cross, also known as the straight right hand, will be one of your main power punches. Muhammad Ali used this punch to great effect when he famously knocked out George Foreman in their 1974 fight in Zaire. When executed correctly, a single landed blow can knock an opponent out.

The mechanics of the right cross are similar to the jab in that they are both far-range punches. However the execution of a right cross is a bit more intricate, and it has a tremendous amount of power because you put your body weight behind it. The dynamic force of the blow is derived from a combination of speed, snap, and thrust.

STEP 1: Start in the fighting stance with your hands up by your face and your elbows in to your body. Keep your chin down and your eyes forward, focused on your opponent. Like the jab, the right cross is a linear punch that snaps straight out and straight back.

STEP 2: When throwing the right cross, make sure to lean forward slightly on your left leg while simultaneously turning your hips toward the bag until they are square to it. Your hips will follow the punch so that everything is moving together. Be careful not to raise one hip up as you turn; they should be even. Keep your knees bent to help you stay level. This enables you to generate power from your legs and waist to maximize the impact.

Rotate your fist as you punch so the impact is with the front two knuckles of your index and middle fingers and your palm is facing downward. Visualize that the punch is landing on your opponent's chin or face. Common mistakes are to cock your arm back before you throw the punch or to do a wind up. The punch should come straight off your chin with no extra movement to ensure maximum force and efficiency. Also, in a fight, you don't want to give away or "telegraph" to an opponent that you are about to strike.

Feel everything thrusting together in a smooth motion. Punch through the target and snap your arm back as you return to your original fighting stance.

LEFT HOOK

The left hook is considered by some to be the deadliest punch in the boxing game. Its fearsome reputation was solidified as the signature punch of boxing great Joe Frazier. Its versatility allows it to be thrown in close quarters or at far range. It can be thrown to the head or as an effective body punch because you can generate a lot of power in small quarters.

When working this punch, think "short and sweet." Remember not to wind up and telegraph it to your opponent; keep it quick and strong.

Due to the dynamics of how the punch is thrown, most of your body-weight is behind the power. As its name implies, the left hook travels towards your opponent in a hooking motion and is aimed at your opponent's lower ribs when in close and at the temple or chin when in range.

STEP 1: Start in the fighting stance with your hands up by your face and your elbows in to your body. Keep your chin down and your eyes forward, focused on your opponent.

STEP 2: Raise your left elbow so it is parallel to the floor, maintaining a 90-degree angle with your upper arm and forearm.

3.3 LEFT HOOK   STEP 1   STEP 2

STEP 3: As you begin to throw your left hook, shift your weight slightly forward onto your left leg and turn your hips by pivoting your left foot on the ball of your foot. Your left heel should actually be off the floor when you deliver the blow.

STEP 4: Make sure your elbow stays up when throwing the left hook, and rotate your fist so your palm is facing down and you hit with the front two knuckles of your index and middle fingers. Use the palm-down position for a left hook to the head.

STEP 5: You can also throw a hook to connect to the body (figure 3.3, step 5 on page 34). When you punch mid-body, your hand position changes so that your palm is facing toward you and your thumb is facing up. The reason for the change in your hand position from a head shot to a body shot is to get better coverage. By turning your palm towards you on a body punch, you adjust the shape of your hand to the shape of the impact area, the rib cage.

UPPERCUT

The uppercut is a very important punch for a boxer in the clinches, where you are fighting very close in and often have continuous body contact or even one boxer holding onto the other to try to keep the opponent too close to punch. The uppercut lets you deliver lots of power in tight quarters. It is the best punch to use when going for the chin or the solar plexus (the pit of the stomach that houses the viscera, including the liver, pancreas, and intestines) or when you're in a situation where there is little or no room to maneuver. The weapon of choice of Mike Tyson, one of the best inside fighters of all time, was the uppercut. Once the starting bell rang, he would get in close and deliver this devastating knockout punch to end matches quickly and definitively.

You can generate so much force with this punch because it carries the momentum from your legs to throw your entire body weight into it. As you throw the punch, your knees straighten, your hips rotate and move upward, and your whole body turns into the blow with a thrusting motion.

STEP 1: Start in the fighting stance (figure 3.4, step 1 on page 36). Drop down slightly with bent knees and lower your right shoulder to drop the right side of your body. You need to give yourself the room to come up with power. When you are on the inside, close to your opponent, the only direction to move is down. Remember to keep the left hand by your chin to protect your head.

STEP 2: Rotate your hips forward while turning your right foot and pivoting on the ball of your foot (figure 3.4, step 2 on page 36). As you turn, straighten your knees. This lifting motion increases the force of the punch. Punch upward, keeping your arm bent at a 90-degree angle. Make contact with the front two knuckles of your index and middle fingers. The uppercut is effective to the body or the head. Aim for a hit square to the chin or the bottom of the rib cage.

STEP 3: After throwing the punch, recoil your body back into the fighting position and pivot your right foot back into your the boxing stance.

For maximum force, focus your punch beyond the contact point. You should feel as though you are punching *through* your opponent. The uppercut *should not* be thrown in a winding motion as this will take your arm away from the front of your body and leave you open to an attack. If your arm is too far out, you will "telegraph" to your opponent what you are about to do and give them the opportunity to block.

Now that you have learned the mechanics behind each punch, you'll be able to incorporate them in your workout and eventually in an actual fight. It will take time and training to perfect your punches and learn whether your strengths lie in the far-range punches, like Muhammad Ali, or in the short-range, inside punches like powerhouses Mike Tyson and Joe Frazier. But offensive moves can only get you so far. You need to be able to defend yourself as well, and we'll discuss how to do that in the next chapter.

CHAPTER FOUR

DEFENSE

efense in boxing is as simple as trying not to get hit. The boxing mantra, "Hit and don't get hit," sounds simple, but there is nothing simple about it. "Not getting hit" takes a lot of practice. If you are going to be fighting in the ring, you will take some shots, but a good defense will prevent a bout from being a round of constant punishment or ending in a knockout.

As an exercise routine, working your defensive moves will teach you boxing as an art form by working your muscles the way they are supposed to be. In return you'll get the full benefit of the exercise and 100 percent output from your body.

In this chapter we'll be learning some basic defense that will then be utilized in the shadow boxing and bag work parts of the workout found in chapters five and seven, respectively. Obviously in a bout this basic defense gets more complicated because your opponent will be throwing combination punches, not individual ones; however, a good defense starts with learning the basics and then practicing them with bag drills and shadow boxing.

We will focus on three main components: *blocking*, *slipping*, and *ducking*. These will be the foundation of your defense, help you stay protected, and give you the ability to "not get hit."

First, let's go over some of the common mistakes made in defense.

- **Not keeping your hands up and your chin down.** If you drop your hands, you create an opening for your opponent's glove to deliver a blow. If your chin is up, it is easier to get underneath to deliver an uppercut.

- **Not keeping your eyes on your opponent.** Always look at the person you are fighting to spot clues as to what he will do next. You can't block something you don't see coming.

- **Not staying on balance.** Proper balance cannot be stressed enough. Not only does it allow you to move in and out as needed, it is the source of your power when you do get to take a shot.

- **Flinching.** Try not to break your stance and shrink away from a punch. Stay defensive and block.

- **Don't reach to block.** Frequently you will see people moving their block *away* from their body in an effort to stop an incoming punch. This actually reduces your guarded area. Keep your guard close.

BLOCKING

The first rule of blocking is to keep your hands up (figure 4.1). Most of the punches that you will block will be absorbed by the forearms, elbows, and shoulders. Although keeping your hands up will automatically defend against most attacks, there are specific ways to block certain punches.

As we go through these, remember to (1) keep your *hands up,* your elbows tucked in close to your body by your ribs, and your chin down, and (2) *keep moving.* Mohammed Ali, the master of not getting hit, had his own saying. The first half of it, as I'm sure you are familiar, was "Float

4.1 BLOCKING STANCE

like a butterfly," signifying that he was agile and always kept moving. Now we'll learn how to block specific punches.

Blocking a Jab

One of the best ways to block this punch is to *catch* the jab as if the punch is aimed for your palm (figure 4.2). When catching the jab, open your left hand slightly, tighten up your left arm, and brace yourself for the blow. You can catch the punch with either your left or your right hand. Which hand you use will depend on which side of your body the blow is aimed. If you can catch your opponent's jab, you will then have the ability to counterpunch. If you have made the catch with your left hand, you would counter with your right and vice versa.

4.2 BLOCKING A JAB

Blocking a Right Cross

There are a couple of ways to block a right cross. One way is to bring the arms up, creating a shield-like position. Your forearms will absorb the impact of the punch. Another way to block the cross is to use a shoulder block (figure 4.3). When the cross is coming toward you, turn your body and catch the punch with your left shoulder. Always block with the shoulder that is closest to your opponent, so it doesn't matter if your opponent is left- or right-handed; your left shoulder will always be closer. Of course, if *you* are left-handed, then it would naturally be your right shoulder. When using the shoulder block, it is very important to remember to keep your chin down so you're not exposed to getting hit.

4.3 BLOCKING A RIGHT CROSS

Blocking a Left Hook

In chapter three when we reviewed punching, you may remember that you can aim the left hook towards the body or the head. To block a left hook, you use a basic right block. When you see the left hook coming, you simply bring your right arm up and tighten up, absorbing the blow with your forearm (figure 4.4 on page 42). How high you raise your block depends on whether your opponent is aiming for your midsection or your head.

Blocking Uppercuts

To block an uppercut, intercept your opponent's blow with a glove block (figure 4.5). Lower your right or left glove with your palm facing the floor and your elbow up so that your forearm and upper arm form a 90-degree angle parallel to the floor in front of your chest. Tighten the muscles in your blocking arm to prepare for the force of the interception. Tightening is the key to the block to ensure that you stop the uppercut. If you are not tight, the punch will blow past your block and connect with your chin. Use either your right or left arm in this block, depending on which arm the punch is thrown with. A right uppercut is blocked with your left arm and vice versa.

Blocking Body Shots

To block shots to your body, use a right forearm block or a left forearm block, depending on which side of the body your opponent is attacking (figure 4.6). To perform the block correctly, keep your arm bent in

4.5 BLOCKING UPPERCUTS

4.6 BLOCKING BODY SHOTS

your guard position and lower your forearm so that your elbow is down over your ribs. Be sure not to reach away from your body with your arm; keep it in close to your ribs and turn slightly *away* from the blow to avoid the full impact. If you turn *into* the blow, you will be increasing the force of the punch. Even with the block you will still feel the punch, but the forearm block will protect your body and absorb most of the power the blow.

SLIPPING

Slipping is a quick movement of the head to the right, left, or back to evade attacks. The purpose of slipping is to get out of the way of your opponent's straight-on attack punches, like a jab or a right cross, and sometimes for a left hook. Mike Tyson was famous for his slipping, and Floyd Mayweather rarely got hit because he was almost constantly using this defensive move. Performing the slip correctly not only gives you the ability to evade your opponent's punch, it can also give you the ability to open your opponent up for a counterpunch. It will be one of your best forms of defense because by slipping, you avoid getting punished and tired out by your opponent. Even an effectively blocked punch can still hurt and tire you out, so the more contact you can avoid, the better off you will be.

When slipping, move your torso from the waist up in a side-to-side, "windshield wiper" motion. Move enough to slip the punch but *don't overexaggerate* the motion because you don't want to waste energy or lose your balance, and you especially don't want to miss the opportunity to counterattack.

Slipping a Jab

Generally when slipping a jab, it is best to slip to the outside of your opponent's punch (figure 4.7). This will make you harder to hit and will

give you a great position to counter, as you will be at his side, which is relatively unprotected.

Slipping a Right Cross

To slip a right cross, move your body slightly to the left (figure 4.8 on page 46). Make sure to always keep your eyes on your opponent and keep your hands up.

Slipping a Left Hook

Unlike when slipping the straight-line attacks, you will need a different slip for the left hook since the punch will come at you from the side. Instead of a side motion, you will need to lean your torso *back* about six inches, just enough to get your head out of the way of the punch. Be sure that you only lean back a few inches and that you keep your arms up and your knees bent, and stay on balance to make sure you're in position to counter.

DUCKING

Ducking is similar to slipping in that it is another way for you to move your head away from your opponent's punch and, at the same time, create a good position for a counterpunch. However, instead of a side or back movement away from the punch, ducking is a *downward* movement. In a fight, use both slipping and ducking so that you aren't predictable and so that you can confuse your opponent by using different evasions. Ducking is a good setup for a body shot counterpunch because it positions you on the side of your opponent.

To duck, bend your knees slightly so that you lower your head just enough to evade the punch (figure 4.9, step 1). As you straighten your knees again, do not come straight up but rather at an angle so that your body makes a V-shaped motion (step 2). This ducking motion actually takes you *under* your opponent's arm (step 3), so that when you come up

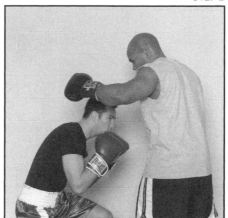

you will be either to the outside or inside of your opponent's stance (step 4), depending on the punch you ducked and which way you moved.

To practice this movement, stand in front of a bar that is at chin height (such as playground equipment or a friend holding his arm out in front of him, or use your wraps and tie each end to something at the right height). With your hands up in guard position and your feet in the fighter stance, practice moving from one side of the object to the other by ducking under it and popping up on the other side.

Your decision to come up on the outside or inside depends on what type of punch you are evading. For example, when evading a right-handed punch, either a right cross or a right hook, to the head, you would duck to the left and come up on the outside of your opponent. Most ducking will bring you up on the outside of your opponent. This means that you will be at his side with both of his shoulders in front of you. It is more difficult for your opponent to get to you from this position because he will have to move away in order to reach you. Since you are in a relatively unguarded area of your opponent's torso, you will likely have an opening for a counterpunch. Your best counterpunch will be a hook to his torso or head. If you follow the mechanics of the motion, as you come up from the duck your torso turns to the outside; this positions you well to turn into the hook and deliver it with a lot of power. It is also possible to deliver a left uppercut to the chin from the outside, although this shot can be a little more challenging.

To evade a left punch to the head, such as a jab, you would duck to the right. This positions you to your opponent's inside, in front of his body and in front of both of his arms. From here, you can counterpunch with a right cross or a right hook to either the head or body, or you can go under your opponent's left arm to deliver an uppercut to the chin.

In your workout sessions, as well as in the ring, you will use both slips and ducks. A general rule is that slips are best against straight-line attacks while ducking works with any punch directed to the head. However, you should be slipping during an entire match so that your head is a constantly moving target. Mix in ducking when you need to in order to evade a punch but also to be unpredictable, and thereby harder to hit. And don't forget: *Always keep those hands up*, because if you don't evade the punch successfully you can at least block it.

CHAPTER FIVE

WARM-UP

It is essential to warm up your muscles before exercising. As you move, blood flow increases to your muscles, which also raises their temperature. Warmer muscles are less prone to injury, and over time your flexibility increases. While athletic activity is beneficial to your body, it can be particularly hard on joints and muscles if your body has not been sufficiently primed for rigorous movement.

A boxer's warm-up consists of three types of activity that prepare the body for the specific rigors of the sport. In this chapter we'll explain the benefits of dynamic stretching, jumping rope, and shadow boxing, and review specific exercises for these areas.

DYNAMIC STRETCHING

The first activity in your warm-up repertoire is stretching. It should be done first to loosen your body for the other exercises. While most people know that stretching is about priming the muscles, this is only half the story. Stretching helps joint mobility as well. Dynamic, or three-dimensional, stretching is all about doing motions that will "oil" the joints while simultaneously getting the muscles warmed up.

What does "oil the joints" mean? Remember how blood flows through a moving muscle to warm it up? A different process happens in the joints because they are surrounded by cartilage and so don't receive a flow of blood. Joint movement stimulates the nervous system and causes the release of synovial fluid. This fluid carries oxygen and nutrients to the cartilage and lubricates the joints. So, the beginning of a warm-up is a great place to activate your body in this way. Once your nervous system has been primed, your body will be ready for movement. Over time and with practice, this nervous system stimulation will help you increase your reaction time and your range of motion. Looking after your joint mobility will ensure better health and strength.

It is important to note that with all of the stretches that follow, the object is to activate the joints and warm up the muscles; the goal is *not* to increase your flexibility right away. Although it is recommended that dynamic stretching is done in sets of eight to twelve repetitions, if you are experiencing pain or discomfort, modify or stop the stretch. Also, for maximum benefit, these exercises should be performed in a *smooth, controlled manner.* You should not be bouncing or jerking in order to reach a certain point of stretch. That may result in your muscles tightening instead of loosening up.

Lastly, your breathing should be natural throughout. Check yourself from time to time to make sure you are not holding your breath. Optimal breathing is nasal inhalation and oral exhalation—breathe in through your nose and out through your mouth.

Now for the stretching exercises—starting at the top.

HEAD AND NECK

Side to Side

Stand with your feet slightly apart and your hands at your sides. Moving only your neck and keeping your chin level, turn your face gently to the

5.1 SIDE TO SIDE   STEP 1

STEP 2

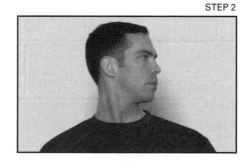

STEP 3

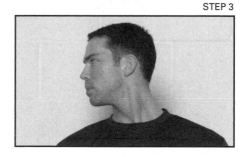

right so that your chin lines up with your shoulder. Then slowly turn your face back over to the left side as far as you can but not further than where your chin lines up with your shoulder. Repeat four times to each side.

Up and Down

Moving only your neck, tilt your head back so that you are looking at the ceiling. Be careful to lift your chin only as far as is comfortable. Do not strain. Then look down and bring your chin toward your neck. Repeat four times.

5.2 UP AND DOWN STEP 1 STEP 2

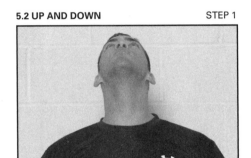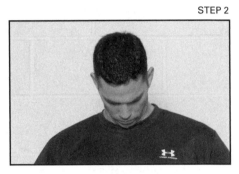

Ear to Shoulder

Bring your right ear down over your right shoulder. This exercise is to stretch the neck, so don't raise your shoulder—keep it relaxed. After a few seconds, raise your head up and do the same on the left side. Repeat four times.

5.3 EAR TO SHOULDER STEP 1 STEP 2

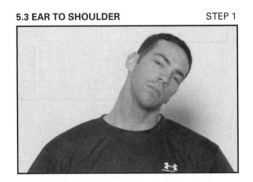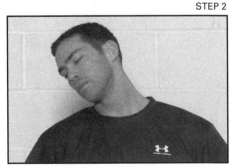

Head Circles

Rotate your head as if you were drawing a circle with your chin. Start over your right shoulder, continue to roll your head on your neck, facing up as though drawing on the ceiling with your chin, then down toward your left shoulder, and finally to your chest. Repeat the motion going in the opposite direction. Do two rotations each way.

5.4 HEAD CIRCLES   STEP 1

STEP 2

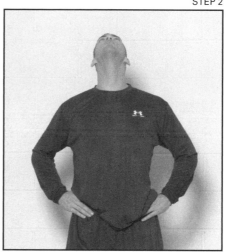

STEP 3

SHOULDERS AND ARMS

Small Arm Circles

Stand with your arms outstretched to both sides at shoulder height. Make small circular motions with your entire arm. Rotate forward for eight counts, then backward for eight counts.

5.5 SMALL ARM CIRCLES

Large Arm Circles

Repeat the arm rotations from the previous exercise but with larger circles, about two feet in diameter. Rotate forward for eight counts, then backward for eight counts.

HIPS

Hip Rotations

Stand with your legs hip width apart and your hands on your hips. Isolate your hip by gently pushing your hip out to the right while keeping

5.6 HIP ROTATIONS

STEP 3

STEP 4

your torso and legs as still as possible. Continue to isolate your hip as you rotate it to the front, to the left, and then to the back. Do four rotations to the right, and then repeat to the left.

LEGS AND FEET

Knee Rotations

Stand with your legs together, your feet about one inch apart. With your knees slightly bent, bend over at the waist so that your hands rest lightly on your kneecaps. Imagine drawing a circle with your knees starting to the right. Do four circles to the right, then repeat to the left.

5.7 KNEE ROTATIONS   STEP 1

STEP 2

STEP 3

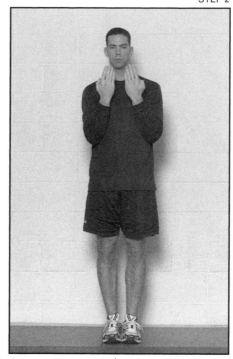

WHOLE BODY

Toe Touch

STEP 1: Stand with your feet together and your arms over your head, straight up over your relaxed shoulders, with your palms flat and facing forward.

STEP 2: As you bend forward from the waist to a 90-degree angle, lower your arms by bending your elbows

alongside your body. Your elbows should be close to your body and your palms facing each other.

STEP 3: Keeping your back at the 90-degree angle, stretch your arms out to touch the floor with your palms now rotated toward your body.

STEP 4: Reverse the motion by first bending your arms and returning your elbows to your ribs with your palms facing each other. Then straighten your body to the standing position as you raise your arms back above your head with palms forward.

* * *

This exercise is about incorporating active movement to stretching. Remember to rotate your palms as you move through the stages of the exercise so that you are moving your joints.

Repeat this exercise ten times.

Side-to-Side Stretch

STEP 1: Stand with your legs slightly wider than shoulder width apart. Rest your left hand on your hip. Reach over your head with your right hand.

STEP 2: Bend your body to the left as if you were pulling yourself by your right hand. The focus of the gentle pull should be *up* and *over* toward the far wall. *Reach long.* Your arm should be over your head at a 45-degree angle. Be sure to keep your chest square and your shoulders back.

STEP 3: Hold for a split second at the height of your stretch, then return to the upright posture and repeat on the other side.

Waist Twist

STEP 1: Stand with your feet a little more than hip width apart. Hold your arms at a 90-degree angle with your elbows bent out so they form a loose circle in front of your chest.

STEP 2

5.10 WAIST TWIST

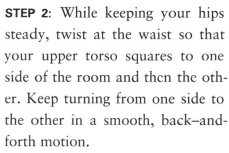

STEP 2: While keeping your hips steady, twist at the waist so that your upper torso squares to one side of the room and then the other. Keep turning from one side to the other in a smooth, back–and–forth motion.

One twist is turning to both the right and left sides. Do ten twists.

Leg Stretch

STEP 1: Begin with your legs in a wide stance, about double your shoulder width apart.

STEP 2: Drop down over your right side by bending your right leg and putting your hands on the floor in front of you. Keep your right foot flat on the floor; do not lift your heel. Your left leg should be straight out to the side with your foot in a flexed position (toes facing the ceiling).

STEP 3: While maintaining the low posture, shift to the left side so that you are over a bent left leg with your left foot flat on the floor. Your right leg is now straight with your foot flexed.

STEP 4: Repeat switching from side to side ten times, five times per side.

5.11 LEG STRETCH   STEP 1

JUMPING ROPE

A boxer's warm-up should always include some rope jumping. Not only does it get your heart rate up and improve your endurance, but it also prepares your body in ways that are specific to boxing. Jumping rope develops coordination by requiring simultaneous multiple movements. It's great for footwork because it gets you accustomed to shifting your weight quickly and easily while you simulate the forward, backward, and side–to-side movements in a fight. Since jumping is done primarily on the balls of your feet, you can practice maneuvering on that part of the foot which, as a boxer, you must use to move quickly and stay light and agile in the ring. Also, jumping rope helps you learn to get a rhythm going and to stay relaxed, which are definite advantages when you are up against an opponent.

Before we get started with the different jump rope exercises, let's review some of the body basics to ensure an effective session. First, *stay relaxed*. If you tense up, you will tire more quickly and you may end up straining your muscles. Next, *drink plenty of water* before and after jumping rope, as well as between sets. Jumping requires a lot of energy and it will make you sweat. Keep yourself hydrated to avoid getting dizzy and lightheaded. *Be aware of your wrists*; they should be straight and at ease, not bent at an angle. Lastly, *pace is important*. Try to keep a nice, steady pace throughout the jumping session. The only time the pace will vary is during the last thirty seconds when you go all out, similar to a runner sprinting at the end of a run.

Figure Eights

Get your body ready before you start jumping rope. The figure eight arm movement (swinging the rope in front of your body in a figure eight pattern) gets you started with a rhythm while you stretch out the upper chest and back muscles. If you don't have a lot of "swing room" where you are doing the exercise, you can do this without the rope as well.

5.12 FIGURE EIGHTS

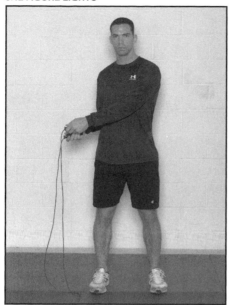

5.13 STANDARD "BUNNY HOP" JUMP

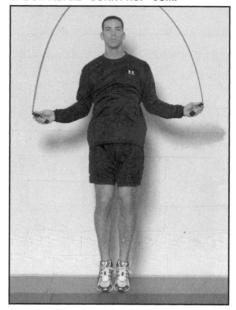

STEP 1: Hold one rope handle in each hand and keep your hands together at chest height.

STEP 2: Keeping your hands together, swing the rope to the right in a circular motion and then over to the left side in another big circle. You will be making a large figure eight in front of your body. The rope will swing out to the sides and you should feel a breeze.

During the jump rope part of your warm-up, the figure eight exercise is a great movement to do if you need a break without losing momentum.

Standard "Bunny Hop" Jump

Keep your feet together and jump lightly one inch off the ground as you swing the rope under your feet. Remember to keep your arms close to your body. You should feel the jump momentum "up" more than the "down." It may help to visualize landing on a piece of glass to help keep that landing nice and light.

One Leg Hop

STEP 1: Lift one leg with the knee bent and hold it as high as you can in front of you. Continue to jump at the same pace as the standard "bunny hop" on just the one leg.

STEP 2: Switch legs and hop. Do ten hops on each leg.

Running in Place

Alternate your legs as if you were running in place while you rotate the rope once for each foot. To make this one really effective, each time you lift a leg, try to get your knee up to waist level or as high as you can. Again, the momentum is in the upward motion, so really try to drive your knees up.

Switch Stance

Starting in a boxer's stance with one foot about shoulder width apart and in front of the other, jump and reverse the front and back feet with each rope rotation.

5.14 ONE LEG HOP

5.15 RUNNING IN PLACE

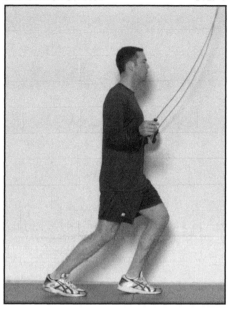

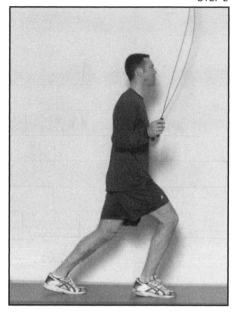

Boxer's Shuffle

While you jump, shift your weight from one foot to the other. When the rope makes its rotation, you will actually be hopping on one foot. This is a shuffle, though, so don't raise your foot more than an inch or so from the floor. Focus on your speed and go as fast as you can.

Heel Kick

While you jump, kick the non-jumping foot back on the first hop and kick forward on the second

5.17 BOXER'S SHUFFLE

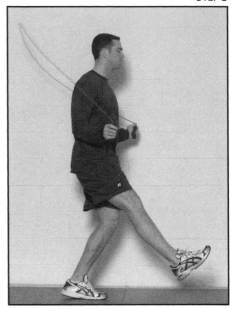

hop. Switch feet after each heel/kick combination so the alternate foot does the heel/kick.

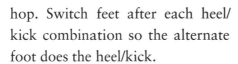

ADVANCED JUMPS

Arm Cross

5.19 ARM CROSS

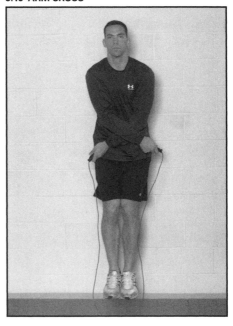

Try this one with the standard "bunny hop" jump. As your arms come in front of you, cross them in front of your chest before the jump, then uncross them back to your sides after the jump.

Doubles

This is like a standard "bunny hop" jump except that the rope makes

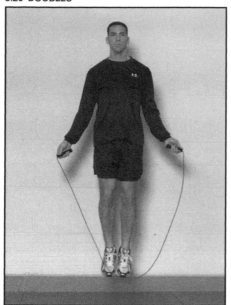

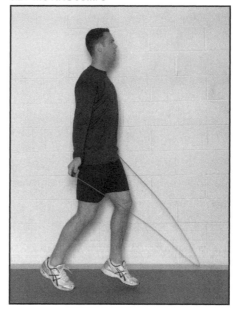

two revolutions for each hop. For success, each jump will have to be a little higher to allow enough time for the rope to get around the extra time. This jump can be alternated with singles, or you can bust out a string of doubles during the final thirty seconds of jump work.

Moving Jumps

Be sure you have at least ten feet of space to do these more advanced jumps.

- **Forward and backward:** Alternate knee lifts while jumping forward about five times on each leg. Then switch direction and alternate knee lifts while moving backward.

- **Side to side:** Begin by moving your right leg in a lateral movement to the right, about a hip width. Follow with your left leg. There should be one rope rotation for each complete step with both feet to the side. Once you have side-stepped five times, reverse direction and make the lateral movement beginning with your left leg and following with your right.

SHADOW BOXING

Shadow boxing, in essence, is a drill that simulates a match with an imaginary opponent. The drill has been compared to movement disciplines like kata in karate or tai chi. The major difference is that unlike these martial art forms, shadow boxing has no set movement routine. Although shadow boxing is considered part of your warm-up, you are also practicing your boxing techniques.

This can be done anywhere there is some space, but shadow boxing in front of a mirror is best because you can check your form and use yourself as a target. Since *you* are the imaginary opponent, stand where you can see yourself, but be sure that you are far enough away that you will not accidentally come in contact with the mirror.

The key to successful shadow boxing is *visualization*. Create in your mind the idea that you are in the ring. This mindset will help you keep your intensity, prepare your body and mind for training, and make this drill a whole lot of fun.

Start off slowly; give your mirror image a few jabs, making sure that you keep good form. Move around as if you were in a real fight. Think about your footwork, moving forward and back while throwing jabs; move side–to-side while practicing slipping, ducking, and blocking (see chapter four). The more you get into it, the more you will get out of it. Throw a punch to your mirror chin, move to the side, or strategize your next move. You can even pretend that you get hit. Some people love the adrenaline rush that they feel when they get hit in a match and use that feeling in their workouts. Pretending to get hit also helps you to remember your blocking moves. Once you have the hang

of it, you can progress to using some of the punch combinations that we will review in the next chapter.

Stay relaxed, crank up the music, and be creative. Begin with one or two three-minute rounds and work up to three three-minute rounds with one minute of rest between each round.

That completes a boxer's warm up session. Now it's training time.

CHAPTER SIX

COMBINATION PUNCHES

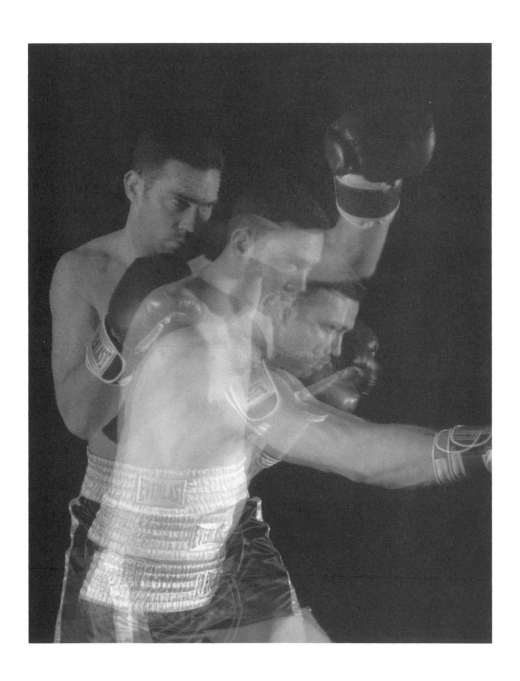

A combination punch is a series of two or more punches. It can be as basic as two of the same punch, such as a double jab, or as intricate as five punches delivered with precision timing. Learning to execute combination punches is really the heart of boxing because the combinations allow you to create openings in your opponent's defense and land the punches.

The training for learning combination punches simply requires a lot of repetition. Your body needs to learn the *flow dynamic* of the different combinations. Flow dynamic means the mechanics of the punches, or how your body moves and adjusts from one punch to the next. Not only must the mechanics be technically correct but fluid, quick and smooth without hesitations between them. Learning the flow dynamic can help you overcome some common problems.

One problem is that it is easy to lose the form of each punch and get sloppy in your combinations. When you do not punch effectively, by not maintaining form, you are creating openings for your opponent. Another problem is that it can be difficult to maintain your balance while moving and adjusting your body and throwing your weight into a punch. Drilling will get your body at ease with all this dynamic movement and keep you from crossing your feet, which immediately takes away your balance. Learning flow dynamic makes throwing combination punches second nature. They have to be instinctual in a fight situation, and, as with most things in life, that means *practice, practice, practice.*

In a fight, you cannot limit yourself to any set movement because you cannot predict a dynamic situation. If the combination punches are intuitive, you can adjust according to the situation. Think of punches as your vocabulary. The more words—or punches—you know, the better you are able to string together effective combinations.

Although punches can be put together in a variety of ways, there are standard combinations in boxing that will be your foundation. Keeping with the vocabulary analogy, the standard one-two jab/cross punch is like the simple words *ball* or *red*. A child learning to read masters these common words first and then reads them without effort as he progresses to more difficult text. Once you have mastered the basic punches, you can then throw them naturally in a fight with little effort.

Feeling comfortable with the combination punches is only half the battle. You will learn apply them effectively in a fight through sparring drills that are discussed in chapter eleven.

BASIC COMBINATIONS

The goal is to put the two punches together in a quick, fluid motion. Your keys to combination punches are: flow and timing.

Let's start with standard combinations that will give you a strong foundation for sparring. As we discussed in chapter three, the jab is a great punch for controlling the distance between you and your opponent in a fight. That is why most punch combinations start with a jab.

Jab / Right Cross

STEP 1: Take a fighter's stance with your left foot forward and jab with your left hand (figure 6.1, step 1 on page 74).

STEP 2: As you recoil the jab, your right arm executes a right cross (figure 6.1, step 2 on page 74). For the timing of the combination, think to yourself "one-two," "one-two" with each set. Be sure that you fire your right hand as your left is recoiling.

Remember that flow is not just the smoothness of your movements. You need to watch your technique as well. Is your right foot pivoting on the right cross? Is your weight on your toes? Is your non-punching hand up by your face? Is your elbow in front of your ribs, not out to the side?

When training, you will need to practice all aspects of distance from your opponent or the bag. The jab is the best way to measure your distance. If you can reach out and hit, you know that you have the right distance to

throw a combination punch effectively. If you are training on a heavy bag, the bag will move as you punch it, which will naturally require you to step in if you are out of range and step back if you are too close. Your footwork, as you move forward and back, should be timed with your blows.

- **Beginner:** Start the repetitions slowly and deliberately until the flow comes together with the form intact. Then mix it up by working the ranges, moving forward and back as the bag movement dictates.

- **Advanced:** Move around the bag as it moves, looking for openings and the best hit range.

Jab / Right Cross / Left Hook

In this combination the left hook is to the body (not the head, where a hook can also be aimed). The secret here is *fluctuation*. By fluctuating from hit-

ting up high (head shot) to hitting low (body shot), you force your opponent to raise or lower his guard. This is how you create openings and opportunities to land a punch.

STEP 1: Take a fighter's stance with your left foot forward. Start with a left jab to the chin (head shot).

STEP 2: As you recoil from the jab, hit the chin again with a right cross (head shot). Remember to pivot on the ball of your right foot as you deliver the punch.

STEP 3: As you recoil from the cross, bend your knees as you pivot toward the right on the ball of your left foot to throw a left hook to the body (figure 6.2, step 3 on page 75). Aim for the side of the body where the lower ribs are (body shot).

- **Beginner:** Start slowly. Practice the 1-2-3 fluid motion while keeping your form. Don't incorporate too much footwork movement at first; focus on the flow, or the continuous motion from one punch to the next. Be sure to maintain the foot pivot for the cross and the knee bend on the hook. Do repetitions until it feels comfortable and it's second nature to throw the combination quickly while maintaining correct positioning throughout the body.

Remember when you throw a hook to the body that the thumb is on the top of your glove toward the ceiling, not toward you as when you throw a hook to the head.

- **Advanced:** Move back before initiating the combination so that you have to step into the jab. As the heavy bag moves, move with it.

Jab / Right Cross / Left Hook / Right Cross

The fluctuation from high punches to the head to a lower punch to the body and then back up high again really creates openings as your opponent is forced to move his blocks. This is a particularly powerful combination if you are going for the knockout punch because after you set up with the jab, you let loose with a lot of body power in the follow-up punches. Finishing with a really good head shot can be devastating to your opponent.

STEP 1: Take a fighter's stance. Step in with a left jab to the chin to set up the combination (head shot).

STEP 2: As you recoil the jab, follow with a right cross to your opponent's chin (head shot).

6.3 JAB / RIGHT CROSS / LEFT HOOK / RIGHT CROSS

STEP 1

STEP 2

STEP 3

STEP 4

STEP 3: Your opponent's defenses are up around the face now, so as you recoil from the right cross, bend your knees and aim the left hook to the side at the lower rib cage (body shot). (See figure 6.3, step 3 on page 77.)

STEP 4: The left hook has now caused your opponent to lower his block either because you have hurt him or because he is blocking (figure 6.3, step 4 on page 77). This sets you up for the right cross to the chin (head shot).

- **Beginner:** Practice the moves slowly to keep the body, legs and arms in good position throughout the transitions. Whether you use a mirror to check your form or hit the heavy bag, *visualize* the target. As you hit up high, picture hitting someone in the chin; as you go down to the body shots, imagine hitting in the ribs.

Remember your timing. Your punches should be coming out as you recoil from the previous punch.

- **Advanced:** Loosen up and move around. Neither the heavy bag nor an opponent is going to stand still for you, so incorporate more footwork. Even when running drills, you can move into the close position to land the punches and move out of range again before beginning the next combination.

Jab / Left Uppercut / Right Cross

This is a great combination to set up for a devastating right cross. Unlike the previous combination punches, this one is all high, so you are really focused on taking your opponent down with a brutal head blow.

STEP 1: Take a fighter's stance. Step in with a left jab to the chin to get in and get close (head shot). Recoil your hand back.

STEP 2: Pivot on your left foot, which will turn your hips toward the right, and use your left hand again to deliver an uppercut directly under the chin.

STEP 1

STEP 2

If the punch is delivered properly, your opponent's head will snap back (head shot).

STEP 3: When the head snaps back, your opponent will have limited vision to what's coming next, so you have perfect cover to follow up with a right cross to the chin (head shot). Pivot on your right foot as you throw the punch.

The uppercut is like a homing device for the right cross—it snaps the chin back to give a dead-on target for the follow-up punch.

STEP 3

How much you use footwork in this combination depends on what your opponent does. If he comes in closer after the jab, you'll have to deliver the uppercut as you step back, and then step forward again as you throw the right cross. Boxing is an intricate and dynamic dance with an opponent; that's why you have to drill these combinations until you are comfortable enough with the flow of your energy and power in different directions to react with split-second timing and not lose your balance.

- **Beginner:** Do this combination in the mirror before moving to the bag. Keep your form through each punch and visualize where on an opponent you are landing the punches.

When you do get to the bag, take it slowly at first. You should feel relaxed throughout the drill.

- **Advanced:** Play around with the movement of the bag as you drill. As discussed, the movement of the bag simulates an opponent and will dictate your footwork. Keep checking the basic form for the sloppiness that creeps in when doing combinations. Are your elbows in? Are you telegraphing (giving away) your next move by lowering your arm or cocking your arm back before the punch? Are you staying on your toes and keeping balanced?

Left Uppercut / Right Uppercut / Left Hook

This combination is all to the body, so it is used when you are on the inside, meaning in close to your opponent. Drilling it will get you comfortable generating power in tight quarters. The key to this combination is *bending your knees*.

With your knees bent, you will be facing your opponent's chest. Make yourself a tough target by literally burying your head in his chest (your hairline makes contact at pectoral level). This way, you will have access to his mid-section while he can only punch down, a direction from which

STEP 2

a punch cannot be delivered with any great power.

STEP 1: Take a fighter's stance. Execute a left uppercut to the solar plexus, the six-pack muscles at the abdomen (body shot).

STEP 2: Go for a right uppercut to the solar plexus again (body shot).

STEP 3: Finally hit your opponent with a left hook to the ribs (body shot).

Using this combination to go to the body so many times in a row

STEP 3

will bring your opponent's arms down to block because it will hurt. This allows you to tire him out and create an opening for a head shot, which you can deliver after this combination is successful.

Fighting close creates other challenges, though. Here are a couple of common mistakes to watch out for:

- **Don't get tense.** A good fighter is equally relaxed on the outside and on the inside. Adrenaline can really pump when close in, so try and stay calm and look for openings. You will not be able keep the flow of the combination punches going if you tense your muscles.

- **Watch your balance.** There is a lot of contact with your opponent when you're close. Your opponent may "hold" you or "hug" you to disable your ability to punch, and then push you back and away. If you aren't low, you can easily get thrown off balance. So drop down and use your center of gravity for leverage and power.

- **Don't stay static.** Keep moving in between combinations. Whether you slip, block, duck, or move your feet, *move* and don't allow yourself to be a sitting target.

  - **Beginner:** Practice staying low with your body close to the bag and your head close to or even touching the bag.

  - **Advanced:** Work on the setup for getting in close. Start a little more than arm's length away from the bag and use your jab as you step in. The jab acts as a decoy, or distraction, which allows you to get close enough to use the body combination.

Double Jab / Left Hook / Left Uppercut / Right Cross

This five-punch combination can use up a lot of energy. In a fight, you can't just throw punches continuously or you will tire out. You need to be smart and pick your shots. With that said, once you have hurt your opponent, that's the time to let loose with this combination and go in for the kill.

STEP 1: Take a fighter's stance. Throw two right jabs in quick succession to the chin (head shot). The first jab should get you in close and the second even closer. It is imperative to throw the jabs with *intensity* to create a distraction and get your opponent to lower his guard to give you the chance to get in real close.

STEP 2: As your second jab is recoiling, bend your knees and throw a left hook to the exposed ribs (body shot). This should prompt your opponent to lower his guard to protect his mid-section.

STEP 3: Throw the fourth punch, a left uppercut under the chin to snap the head back (head shot). Since you are down low when you throw this punch, you will have the power of your legs behind you for real impact (figure 6.6, step 3 on page 84).

**6.6 DOUBLE JAB / LEFT HOOK /
LEFT UPPERCUT / RIGHT CROSS**   STEP 1   STEP 2

STEP 4

STEP 4: Follow the left uppercut with a right cross to finish while the head is still back and your right hand is still out of your opponent's field of vision (head shot).

This is an advanced boxing move, but you can utilize it in training to practice flow and rhythm. Start by practicing in the mirror before you move to the bag. Before long, you'll be enjoying the thrill of throwing combination punches with confidence.

* * *

Combination punching increases your heart rate, muscle tone, and stamina. The better you become at executing combinations, the more you will get out of the bag drills and you'll be able to intensify your workouts. In the ring, the ability to throw multiple combinations is essential. The basic combinations learned in this chapter can be the foundation to developing your own combinations based on your best punches. For example, if you have a great left hook, you may want to incorporate that punch more frequently. Learning the basics and then creating combinations based on your individual strengths will be part of your development as a fighter.

CHAPTER SEVEN

BAG WORK

Whether you are looking to get into the ring or simply to get a great workout with the thrill of boxing, working the bags is both essential and stimulating. There are three types of bags that we will be working with: the heavy bag for developing power and opponent simulation; the speed bag for developing coordination and speed; and the double end bag for developing accuracy and agility.

HEAVY BAG

The heavy bag is integral to a great boxing workout because it gives the best simulation of being in the ring with an opponent. As with a real life opponent, it moves in different directions as you work with it, so you have to utilize both your offensive skills to keep within range and your defensive skills to avoid and block. Visualization really helps bring it all together, so imagine your bag as a sparring partner and get a placement for where the chin, ribs and stomach would be. The bag has some heft to it so you will feel every punch. This is what helps you develop the power in your punches.

When first starting with the heavy bag, take it slowly to give you some time to understand distance with the heavy bag. To develop this understanding we will be going through three kinds of heavy bag drills: the single punch drill, the footwork movement drill, and the free round drill.

Single Punch Drills

This drill involves repetition to both perfect the technique and acquire a more powerful punch. We will review using the jab, right cross, uppercut and hook (see chapter three), although you may choose to work on just one of them in a workout session.

STEP 1: Stand in front of the bag in your fighting stance at punch distance (figure 7.1, step 1 on page 88).

STEP 2: Start by working one type of punch while maintaining form (figure 7.1, step 2 on page 88). Develop a rhythm by punching at a steady pace.

Jab

Start with a single punch, then, after you are comfortable with that, work on double and triple jabs. This means that you fire your punches with a different rhythm. For example, a single punch is *punch-hold-punch-hold*, an even beat rhythm. During the *hold* beat, your hand should be in guard position. A double jab is *punch-punch-hold*. A triple jab is *punch-punch-punch-hold*. Throw a lot of jabs. They are the key to boxing.

As the heavy bag moves, make sure that you maintain the proper distance. If you get too far away to reach the bag with your punch, step forward and jab the bag while moving forward. If you get too close to the bag, step back while you jab. Overall, this drill is for punches, not footwork, so if the bag starts swinging out of range and you are moving a lot, steady the bag so that you can remain in one spot as much as possible.

Right Cross

Start by making sure you have the right distance for your right cross, or straight right hand attack. So that you don't hyperextend your arm, spend some time learning your own distance from the target. With practice you will be able to measure the correct distance by sight in a split second. Until then, pay attention to how far away the bag looks each time you punch. A general rule is that if you can reach your target with a jab, you are at a good distance to throw a right cross. Don't forget to pivot your right foot and hips to the left as you execute the right cross and always hit with the front two knuckles. Once you feel comfortable, don't be afraid to put some power behind that punch. When the bag swings towards you, the right cross should be powerful enough to stop it cold. Visualize yourself stopping a charging opponent.

Left Hook

For the left hook, you need to be in close to the heavy bag. The left hook can be to either the head or the body, so practice on both parts as visualized on the bag. To maintain good form, remember to pivot the front foot and hips to the right while simultaneously turning the hand to hit with your front two knuckles. Don't forget that you are simulating a fight, so when you work your punches, maintain your defensive posture by keeping your guard up with your non-punching hand and your chin down.

Uppercut

Stay close to the bag and keep your knees bent. Drive the uppercut to the center of the bag using your front two knuckles. Do not swing wildly because it gives your opponent an open shot. And remember to snap your punches back so that you keep your hands up and ready on defense.

Footwork Movement Drills

The purpose of this drill is to maintain your stance and balance while moving and staying close to the bag. There are two motions that we will work on: forward and back, which will enable you to maintain the proper distance in a fight; and side to side, which is a defensive move used to evade your opponent while you create an opening in his defense. (Step 1 is for both drills and Step 2 is broken down for each motion.)

STEP 1: Stand about five inches away from the heavy bag in a fighting stance. Stay on the balls of your feet. Since this is a footwork drill, keep your arms up in guard position by your chin. Push the bag with your hands so that it swings directly away from you and toward you, reaching about a 25-degree angle with each swing. Return your arms to guard position.

STEP 2 (FORWARD AND BACK): The goal of the drill is to maintain that five-inch distance between you and the bag by stepping forward as it swings away from you and stepping back as it swings toward you. To keep up you may need to double step, or take two quick steps in succession rather than one big step. Double stepping may be necessary to make sure that your stance doesn't exceed the width of your shoulders. Too long a stride means you are not in the proper boxing stance and you will lose proper weight distribution and, therefore, your balance. When the bag slows, reach out and give it another shove to get it moving again.

7.2 FOOTWORK MOVEMENT DRILLS   STEP 1

Repetition: Three-minute round.

STEP 2 (SIDE-TO-SIDE): The drill is for you to get out of the way of the bag by moving to the side. Start by

stepping to the right of the bag as it comes towards you. When stepping to the right, move your right foot first, followed by your left. You are now facing the side of the bag at a 45-degree angle from where you started. As the bag swings back, return to your starting position. Again, keep pushing the bag as needed to maintain the swing.

Repetition: Alternate five steps to the right and five steps to the left for a three-minute round.

Free Round Drills

This is a challenging endurance drill because you will be throwing a lot of strong punches. The objective is to simulate a sparring match where, instead of working on one thing as you did in the previous drills, you put everything together (figure 7.3 on page 92).

STEP 1: Stand in front of the bag in your fighting stance at punch distance.

STEP 2: Start by throwing a one-two punch (jab / right cross), then step to the side to get out of the way. While on the side of the bag, go for any side shots before you move back to the front.

7.3 FREE ROUND DRILLS

Maintain a constant flow of movement with footwork and slips and ducks with your head and body as you continuously throw different punches and combinations. Use the skills you work on in shadow boxing (see page 68) against the bag.

Here are some tips to remember:

- When you are on the outside of the bag (at least an arm's length distance from your target), you will mainly be using your straight punches, which are the jab and cross.

- When on the inside (less than an arm's length distance to the target), work on your close-range punches like the hook and uppercut.

- Always keep your focus and form. Don't get sloppy.

- Maintain your defensive attitude by keeping your guard up and using elbow blocks against the bag. Raise your block to protect your head and lower it to protect your abdomen.

- Visualize the bag as an opponent and throw your punches with accuracy.

- Adjust your punches and keep up your footwork the whole time to maintain positioning and space. If the bag gets too far away, you can't punch it. If it gets too close, it is akin to getting punched in the ring. Although don't fool yourself; the bag won't hit you like an opponent will.

Repetition: Three-minute round.

SPEED BAG

The main purpose of this bag is to develop speed and timing. It does this by helping you work on your coordination and your split-second response time. It is also a great workout for your arms because you are holding them up for the entire round. Since we are not going for power, and the bag is small, you will not wear your gloves for these drills. Instead, wear just your wraps or the glove wrap. Before you begin, make sure that the bag is positioned so the bottom of it is level, or within two inches, of your chin. Here are the basics of how to hit the speed bag.

Beginner Single Punch Drills

STEP 1: Stand in front of the bag with your feet shoulder width apart and your knees slightly bent. You will be drilling with both arms, but for now, the arm that you are not using to punch with should be up in guard position. Start with your right elbow up at a 90-degree angle in front of your chest. Your hand should be lightly fisted with your palm facing the floor, your thumb toward your face, and your knuckles to the side wall. Hit the speed bag with the *side* of your hand, not your knuckles.

STEP 2: Start *slowly*. This will be very tricky at first, so don't get frustrated. Punch the bag with the outside of your fist, then bring your arm back to the starting position via a circular motion; your fist will be making fluid circles in front of you as you reach out and connect with the bag, then down out of the bag's way and back up to the starting position.

STEP 3: Once you get the motion down, work on developing a rhythm with the bag. Each time you hit the bag it will bounce off the platform above it. A beginning rhythm of bounces to punch should be a count of four. For example: *one*, punch; *two*, the bag hits the platform away from you; *three*, the bag rebounds and hits the platform towards you; and *four*, the bag hits the platform away from you again; then, you go back to *one* with a punch again as the bag comes toward you.

Repetition: Start with the right hand, then with the left hand, then alternating hitting the bag with the right, then left. Do three-minute rounds of each.

Advanced Free Round Drills

Once you are able to hit the speed bag with fluid, rhythmic motions, you can make it even more challenging by mixing up the use of the hands and still maintaining the timing.

Variations you might want to try are:

- Double right, left and double left, right
- Alternating doubles
- Triple right alternating with triple left

Repetition: Three-minute round. As you improve, you will find that you pick up the pace and develop a faster rhythm.

7.4 BEGINNER SINGLE PUNCH DRILLS

DOUBLE END BAG

Roughly the size of a person's head (and simulating the head of your opponent), this challenging bag is tethered to the ceiling and the floor with stretch bands so it moves quickly and in different directions when hit. Learning to master this bag will improve your punch accuracy as well as your defensive slipping skills from dodging the bag as it comes toward you. Start with stationary drills, then move on to the more advanced drills that include footwork. This is not an easy bag to learn, so take it slowly and try not to get frustrated.

Stationary Drills

Take a fighter's stance in front of the bag within your range, close enough to punch it without moving your feet.

Jab

As you throw a jab at the bag, prepare for it to come back at you. Since these are stationary drills, you have three choices: You can slip by moving your head side to side or back, you can duck, or you can block the bag with your arms. Use all of these techniques and mix them up so that you don't set a pattern. Patterns in a fight mean predictability and teach your opponent how and when to get to you. Try to land a few slow jabs as you get used to the motion of the bag and adjust your punch to the movement. The goal is to develop the timing to hit the bag with a consistent rhythm while avoiding getting hit by the bag.

Jab / Cross

Add the cross after the jab.

Jab / Cross / Hook

The goal is to straighten out the bag from the movement created by the first two punches with the hook.

Repetition: Three-minute drill.

***

Proficiency on this bag will take some time to acquire. Keep working on it and remember that your punch will miss the bag a lot. Slow down if you have to; don't rush. The speed and snap will come with practice.

Free Round Drills

Once you are able to hit the double end bag fairly consistently, try adding some movement by angling to the side as we did in the side-to-side heavy bag drill (see page 90). Try a variety of angle sizes: 10 degrees, 20 degrees and 45 degrees. Always keep the double end bag within punching distance.

Move in and out of range as you deliver your jabs. Throw hooks as you step to the side of the bag. You can either mix it up by putting all your punches together or focus on certain combinations, like a double jab/cross, that you feel might need some extra work.

CHAPTER EIGHT

CONDITIONING

onditioning is training your body to accept the physical exertion of an exercise or activity. In boxing, endurance is essential. Your muscles must be conditioned to sustain prolonged use while maintaining effectiveness. Improved endurance, increased strength and greater speed are benefits of conditioning, and all are key components of boxing.

Conditioning is the foundation of your workout and can be likened to the foundations of a house. Without a strong foundation, the house will not stay strong and protective. A weak foundation will crack, and those cracks will cause the entire house to shift and collapse. By adding conditioning to your boxing, you ensure that you have a strong foundation in your upper body so that you can throw a lot of punches, in your lower body where the legs are both a power source and a defensive aide, and in your core where the muscles are your body's armor and allow you to withstand more punishment. Even if you never intend to step into the ring, a conditioning regimen will ensure you have the strength and fitness you desire.

All sports have conditioning exercises that have benefits to that sport. You may be familiar with many of the exercises in this chapter, but we will describe the specific application of the muscle work to boxing. At the end of each exercise is a recommended repetition guide that starts with beginner level (getting in shape) and ends with a professional-athlete level. Anything in between will be your average workout. It is important to pay attention to your body, though, because you may not always equal or improve on the number of repetitions that you completed on your previous workout. The body has good days and bad days. Some days your body is in a mode to push through to a new level, and other days you may feel the need to step it down a notch. Do what feels right for you on a particular day for maximum long-term benefit and fewer injuries.

Before we get to the exercises, let's review some basic technical information about how your muscles work. If you know the theory behind the exercises you will be better able to understand how your body develops stamina and strength. With this knowledge you will be able to tailor your workout to your own needs and get the most out of it.

Skeletal muscles, which are used to create movement, have two types of fibers, the slow-twitch fibers (STF) and the fast-twitch fibers (FTF). The qualities of the two different fiber types affect how your body reacts to physical activity or training. People are born with different degrees of these fibers, and that mixture helps to determine your natural ability. However, you can increase your abilities by stimulating your muscle fibers through specific exercises and motions. A boxer needs to develop both slow- and fast-twitch fibers to be successful in the ring.

The slow-twitch fibers are for endurance. Just as a long-distance runner utilizes these fibers, a boxer also needs them to endure several rounds. Running is a large component of a daily routine to build endurance and develop the STF. Any serious fighter runs on a regular basis with one long-distance run of three to five miles each week. Building up gradually to this level is the best way to maximize health and endurance benefits without overtaxing the body.

The fast-twitch fibers are for short bursts of energy and speed. A boxer's reflexes need to be very fast, and the FTF development is crucial in your ability to slip, duck, and dodge your opponent. Sprinting helps to fine-tune these fibers, so fighters should alternate days of running with days of sprinting 50- to 100-yard dashes. Your conditioning level determines the overall amount of running. Chapter ten has a detailed schedule to help you devise your optimal plan.

Running and sprinting are not your only tools, however. Standard exercises can increase your STF or FTF ability based on the speed at which they are done. Your training will be a combination of endurance and speed. It is important that you alternate the development of the different fibers. Do not work out for speed more than twice a week because you'll run the risk of muscle fatigue and overtraining.

The conditioning exercises are divided into three sections: Upper body, lower body, and core. These areas correlate to the Ultimate Boxing Workout schedule (see chapter ten) where you will be directed to select a different couple of exercises from each section for a day's workout. This means that you will not do all of these exercises in a single workout, but you might incorporate all, or most, of them throughout the week.

UPPER BODY EXERCISES

Pushups

Let's get started with the all-important pushup. Pushups increase your upper body strength, which in turn will increase your punching power. It is very important to know how to do a correct pushup to get the maximum benefit out of the exercise.

STEP 1: Start with your body face down on the floor. Place your hands flat on the floor at chest level slightly wider than shoulder width, but still close to your body. Your legs are close together with your weight on the balls of your feet.

STEP 2: To protect your neck, be sure to hold your head up so that your spine is in a straight line from your head all the way down your back. This includes keeping your butt level with the rest of your body; it should not be higher or lower.

STEP 3: Begin by using your arms to press your body up and down in a controlled motion. Do not allow your body to touch the floor during your down motion.

Remember that quality is more important than quantity, so keep your form throughout.

Pushup With Medicine Ball

Start in the normal pushup position, but with your right palm pressing on the top of a small, 8-pound medicine ball (your left palm is still on the floor). Keep balanced on the ball as you do the pushup repetitions, then switch and do the same number of pushups with the ball under your left palm. Elevating only one side at a time strengthens

8.2 PUSHUP WITH MEDICINE BALL

your back and shoulder muscles in a slightly different way and improves your balance.

Pushup With Step

Use an exercise step or the bottom step of a staircase. First put your feet on the step and your hands on the floor in the normal pushup position. Lower yourself to the floor and up from this position.

8.3 PUSHUP WITH STEP   STEP 1

STEP 2

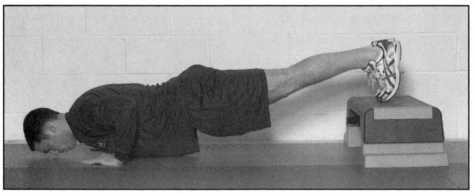

Reverse the configuration so that your hands are on the step and your feet are on the floor in the normal pushup position. Lower your face to the step and up from this position.

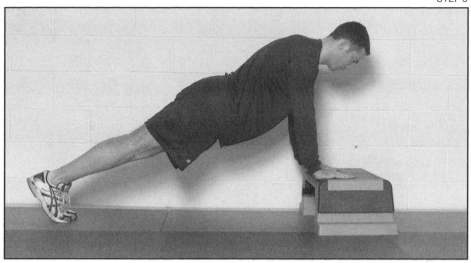

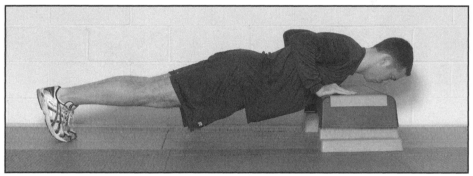

REPETITIONS (WORK YOUR WAY UP):

- **Beginner:** Four sets of five pushups.
- **Advanced:** Four sets of twenty-five pushups.

Medicine Ball Exercises

In addition to adding the medicine ball to most of the conditioning exercises, there are several exercises that are specific to it. Using the ball tones the arms and helps build arm endurance for longer bouts. Any of the ball exercises that involve turning the body are specifically beneficial to boxing because they tone the oblique muscles on the sides of the abdomen, which are protector muscles.

Chest Pass

STEP 1: Stand about 3–4 feet away from a wall (or from a partner) with your feet about hip width apart. Hold the ball at chest height.

STEP 2: Toss the ball off the wall and catch it at chest height (figure 8.4). If you are working with a partner, toss back and forth to each other.

The key is to *explode* on the chest pass to simulate a punch.

REPETITIONS:
- **Beginner:** Ten to fifteen times with a 10-pound ball.
- **Advanced:** Three or four sets of twenty-five with a 20-pound ball.

Shoulder Press

STEP 1: Stand with your feet hip width apart while holding the ball at chest level.

STEP 2: Extend your arms in front of you (figure 8.5). Hold for a second, and then return them to your chest.

Be sure to keep your shoulders relaxed. Don't hyperextend your arms or lock your elbows as you extend straight out; keep them slightly bent so you don't hurt yourself.

8.4 CHEST PASS

8.5 SHOULDER PRESS

8.6 BICEP CURL

REPETITIONS:

- **Beginner:** Ten to fifteen times with a 10-pound ball.
- **Advanced:** Three or four sets of twenty-five with a 20-pound ball.

Bicep Curl

STEP 1: Stand with your feet hip width apart while holding the ball at chest level. Place your palms underneath the ball and keep your elbows close to your body.

STEP 2: Lower your arms by straightening your elbows and holding for a second before curling up again (figure 8.6). Be sure to keep your elbows close to your body.

REPETITIONS:

- **Beginner:** Ten to fifteen times with a 10-pound ball.
- **Advanced:** Three or four sets of twenty-five with a 20-pound ball.

Bicep Curl With Chest Toss

Stand 3–4 feet away from a wall. Each time you raise the ball to your chest, bounce it off the wall and catch it at chest level. Alternate curl and toss.

Tricep Press

STEP 1: Stand with your feet hip width apart. Hold the ball over your head with your arms straight.

8.7 TRICEP PRESS   STEP 1   STEP 2

STEP 2: Lower the ball behind your head by bending your elbows. Keep your elbows close to your temples. Repeat slow bending and straightening.

REPETITIONS:

- **Beginner:** Ten to fifteen times with a 10-pound ball.
- **Advanced:** Three or four sets of twenty-five with a 20-pound ball.

Tricep Press With Chest Toss

Stand 3–4 feet away from a wall or partner. Each time you straighten your arms, bring them back to your chest and do a chest toss against the wall or to a partner.

LOWER BODY EXERCISES

Squats

Believe it or not, a lot of a boxer's power comes from his legs. During those times in the ring when you're tired or hurt, you're going to need strong

8.8 SQUATS STEP 1 STEP 2

legs, and you'll appreciate all the conditioning that you have. Squats will give legs that extra power.

STEP 1: Stand with your feet a little wider than shoulder width apart with your toes pointed outward at a 45-degree angle, knees slightly bent (figure 8.8, step 1 on page 109). Keep your hands stretched out in front of your body to help counterbalance your weight.

STEP 2: Slowly bend your knees, lowering your hips toward the floor (figure 8.8, step 2 on page 109). Keep your back as straight as possible, your shoulders back (not rounding forward), and your chin level to the floor with your eyes focused straight ahead.

STEP 3: Bring your hips as low as you can but no lower than your knees. Keep your back straight as you come up and return to a standing position.

Squat With Medicine Ball
Hold the ball at chest level with your elbows bent and the ball almost resting on your chest. Do a squat.

REPETITIONS:

- **Beginner:** Four sets of ten squats.
- **Advanced:** Four sets of twenty-five squats.

Lunges
As mentioned before, the primary source to generate power in the ring is a strong lower body. Lunges are a great way to build the strength needed to summon that power. They also simulate the forward motion

8.9 SQUAT WITH MEDICINE BALL

that you make each time you throw a forward punch, step toward your opponent, or step back and duck. Exercises that simulate ring moves will condition your body to that movement. They will also condition your mind to be in the fight. If you can make the moves without having to think, your mental focus can be on your opponent. Your body knows the drill, so to speak.

STEP 1: Stand in a fighter's stance with your feet shoulder width apart and your hands on your hips.

STEP 2: Take a long, smooth step straight forward (about double your shoulder width). You don't want to land flat footed; take the time to feel your heel touch first and then your toe as your foot comes down.

STEP 3: Bend your back leg so that your knee comes toward the floor and stops about an inch away from the floor but does not touch it. You will be on the ball of your back foot.

8.10 LUNGES   STEP 1   STEP 2

- **Check your front leg.** Your knee should be right over your foot. If your knee extends beyond your toes, your stance is not long enough, and you could injure your knee by overextending.

- **Check your posture.** Your shoulders should be back, your chest out and your back straight. Keep your abs tight to stabilize your body.

- **Control the motion.** *Don't rush.* If you find that your balance is shaky, go more slowly.

STEP 4: Recoil to the starting position by pushing off on your front foot. Repeat on the same leg for full repetition until you switch to your other leg.

Lunge With Medicine Ball

Lunges can be an even more effective punch simulator with the addition of a medicine ball. Start with an 8-pound medicine ball and work up to an 18-pound ball (or 20-pound ball if you are in top shape). Hold the ball in front of your chest, with your elbows bent and close to your body (figure 8.11, step 1). As you lunge, turn your upper body in the direction of the forward leg in a twisting-from-the-hips/pivot motion (figure 8.11, step 2). As you recoil to the starting position, return to the face-forward position. As you alternate legs, alternate the way you turn your body. Do ten lunges on the right leg before switching to the left, or, if you prefer, alternate from right to left with each lunge.

Moving Forward Lunge

Alternate legs with each lunge as if you were walking. Instead of returning to the starting position, as you move up, bring the back leg forward and go straight into the lunge on the alternate side. Your arms can be on your hips, in a fight-ready position, or holding a medicine ball for an additional challenge.

Backward Lunge

This is a more advanced move, but it mirrors a boxer's agility in the ring. Instead of moving forward, reach back with your leg. This variation can

be done stationary, where you pull your leg forward after each lunge. But for a real balance challenge, it can also be done moving backward where you alternate from leg to leg in a walking backward motion.

REPETITIONS:

- **Beginner:** Ten lunges off of each leg.

- **Advanced:** Three sets of twenty-five lunges.

CORE EXERCISES

Sit-Ups

Sit-ups are one of the main exercises boxers do for *core strength*. Core strength is important for a boxer to optimize strength, power, speed, agility and quickness. Also, a strong core can protect a fighter from potential injuries because strong muscles form a body armor to protect the ribs and internal organs. Here's how to perform a proper sit-up.

STEP 1: Lie on your back with your knees up and feet flat on the floor.

STEP 2: Your optimal hand position is determined by your abdominal strength.

- **Beginner:** Cross your hands across your chest (figure 8.12).

8.12 SIT-UPS FOR BEGINNERS

8.13 SIT-UPS FOR ADVANCED

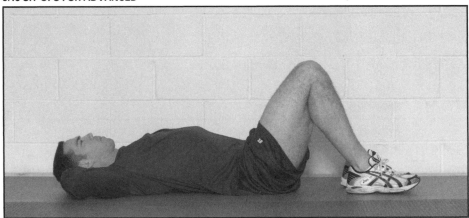

- **Advanced (with greater core strength):** Put your hands behind your head (figure 8.13). If you put your hands behind your head, be sure that you do not pull yourself up with your hands.

STEP 3: As you lift your body up towards your knees, focus on feeling your abs doing the lifting. Regardless of your hand placement or how far you come up, you should have a nice, straight back with *no* rounded shoulders! Do not overcompensate with other muscles.

Keep your neck relaxed and your eyes focused on the ceiling, not your knees, to avoid strain on those muscles. How far up you go is based on your fitness level.

- **Beginner:** Keep your hands folded lightly over your chest and raise yourself halfway (figure 8.14).
- **Advanced:** Keep your hands behind your head (figure 8.15). Keep your neck straight and *do not pull* on your neck; use your stomach muscles to get you up. Raise yourself all the way to a sitting position.

8.14 SIT-UPS FOR BEGINNERS

8.15 SIT-UPS FOR ADVANCED

STEP 4: As you release your body down to the floor, *go slowly*. This is necessary to prevent injury and will maximize the exercise.

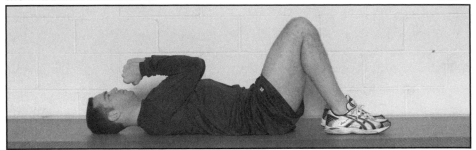

Trademark Boxing Sit-Up

Lie on your back in the starting sit-up position. Put your hands up by your chin in the ready stance, with light fists and elbows in close to body (figure 8.16, step 1). As you come up to the sitting position, use the forward motion to carry you into a seated punch (step 2). You can do a jab, cross or hook. Alternate the hand you punch with each

time you come up (step 3). Return hands to the ready stance position each time you lie down.

You may want to try using the punch combinations this way too. Adding a punch to the sit-up is a great way to tone the sides of your abdomen as well as your arms, and it can make the repetitions more interesting.

You can also have fun with the trademark boxing sit-up by positioning yourself near a bag so that each time you sit up, you can punch the bag. If you have a partner that you work out with, you can punch his open palm as he stands over your knees.

Sit-Up With Medicine Ball

Another variation is to use a medicine ball. Position yourself in the sit-up position with your toes against a wall. Hold the medicine ball in your hands above your head while on the floor (figure 8.17, Step 1). Each time you sit up, keep your hands raised above your head with the ball, then release the ball and bounce it off the wall (Step 2). Catch the ball in front of your chest. As you return to the floor in a smooth controlled motion, move your arms back to the starting position over your head.

8.17 SIT-UP WITH MEDICINE BALL   STEP 1   STEP 2

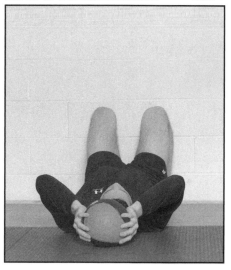 

REPETITIONS:

- **Beginner:** Four sets of twenty-five sit-ups.

- **Advanced:** Four Sets of fifty sit-ups.

Squat Thrusts

This exercise uses mainly core strength but also incorporates your legs and upper body. It builds your endurance and stamina, as well as increases your heart rate. Try a few slowly at first to get the hang of it, and then increase your speed accordingly.

STEP 1: Stand with your feet shoulder width apart and your arms at your sides.

STEP 2: Squat down and get your bottom close to the floor while

8.18 SQUAT THRUSTS   STEP 1

STEP 2

STEP 3

keeping your back straight, your chest out, and your shoulders back. Bend your arms at the elbows with your palms facing each other.

STEP 3: When you are down, place your hands on the ground in front of you and simultaneously thrust out into a pushup position. *Do not* let your back bend up or down. You should have a straight line from your head to your feet. The best way to ensure that you are maintaining posture is to keep your abdominal muscles tight (figure 8.18, step 3 on page 118).

STEP 4: Jump your feet back to the starting position and stand up.

Squat Thrust With Medicine Ball

Hold a medicine ball at chest level in your starting position. Squat

8.19 SQUAT THRUSTS WITH MEDICINE BALL STEP 1

STEP 2

STEP 3

down as with a regular squat thrust (figure 8.19, step 1 on page 119), but instead of putting your hands on the floor, balance your hands on top of the ball (figure 8.19, step 2 on page 119) as you shoot your legs out (figure 8.19, step 3 on page 119). Start with an 8-pound ball and work your way up to 18 pounds.

Squat Thrust With Ball Bounce

Stand 3–4 feet away from a wall, facing it. Do a squat thrust with medicine ball, but each time you come to the standing position, bounce the ball off the wall, catch it at chest height, and then drop into the squat thrust again.

Squat Thrust With Ball Toss

If you work out with a partner, take turns doing the squat thrust with medicine ball with a ball toss. Stand about 3–4 feet apart facing each other. Each time you return to the standing position, throw the medicine ball from chest height toward your partner's chest.

REPETITIONS:
- **Beginner:** Four sets of ten.
- **Advanced:** Four sets of twenty-five.

Side to Sides

STEP 1: Stand with your feet shoulder width apart. Hold the ball with your arms extended out in front of you at chest level, your elbows slightly bent.

STEP 2: Keep your feet and hips stationary as you twist your upper body from left to right.

REPETITIONS:
- **Beginner:** Thirty times (fifteen each side) with a 10-pound ball.
- **Advanced:** Increase the weight of the ball.

8.20 SIDE TO SIDES

CHAPTER NINE

COOL DOWN

The cool down at the end of a workout is beneficial to both the body and the mind. I cannot stress enough the importance of taking the time to fully incorporate relaxation into your routine, whether you are a professional athlete or simply working on a fitness regimen.

Let's talk about the benefits to the body first. The best time to increase flexibility of your muscles is when they are warmed up, which is after a workout. For a boxer, greater flexibility means greater mobility and speed. For example, when you duck, you use your inner thigh muscles, and when you slip, you use the muscles in your waist and torso. The greater flexibility you have in these muscles, the easier you are able to move. Flexibility also affects your range of motion. This is best seen in the extension of a punch. If a boxer's muscles are too tight, he cannot achieve the full power potential of his punches because he cannot fully extend his arms.

The cool down period can also help you learn to control and relax the most important muscle: the heart. When you work out, your heart rate increases. When you cool down, your heart rate decreases because you slow your body down, relax and control your breathing. A boxer needs to be able to take his body from zero to sixty and back to zero again in a match. When you go full out during a round of fighting, your heart rate and respiration rate are elevated, which takes a lot of energy. Once the bell rings for the one-minute break, you must bring those levels down so that you conserve your energy. Take slow, deep breaths to get more oxygen to your muscles and give your body a rest so that you can get out and fight in the next round.

The cool down period is also a good time to reflect on the workout. While you hold your stretches, concentrate on slowing your breathing and relaxing your muscles. At the same time, meditate on the things that you did well in the workout as well as things that you need to improve on. Visualize yourself doing moves better or faster and making improvements. For example, you might think about moving your head more to the side or getting more snap into your jab.

Positive thinking and visualization are important parts of sports psychology. At the Olympic Training Centers there are sports psychologists who help athletes to break through to the next level of ability by improving their mental game. There is a story about a U.S. diving athlete, Laura Wilkinson, who broke three bones in her foot six months before the 2000 Olympic Games in Sydney. She was unable to physically train for two months, so instead she spent several hours each day reviewing all her dives in her head. She visualized everything step by step, turn by turn, and saw herself making the adjustments that she knew she needed to make. She visualized herself diving beautifully. Apparently the technique helped because she went on to win the event. Although boxing does not have a tradition of meditative contemplation like many Eastern martial arts such as karate and tai chi, the practice can be just as beneficial and really can improve your game.

In this chapter we'll go through some specific exercises that will target all areas of the body and help you reduce stress, build a healthier heart, increase flexibility, and learn respiratory control.

BREATHING

But first we need to address breathing. Even though it is something you have done every moment of your life without much thought, how you breathe can greatly affect the value of your cool down.

For a deep breath, fill up your abdomen first (imagine filling your stomach with air), then feel the air fill your lungs. If you are not used to taking a full breath, practice it first by lying on your back, flat on the floor. Rest one hand gently on your abdomen and breathe in. You should feel your stomach rise up as you inhale like a balloon filling up. Strangely, many people suck their stomachs *in* during a big inhale. You don't want this—you want the balloon. All inhalations and exhalations should be from the nose, not the mouth. Practice these deep breaths. Breathe into your abdomen, and then fill up your lungs, before exhaling slowly from the lungs first, then your abdomen. You should feel a wave-like sensation with each breath. Deep, full breathing is the best for the cool down exercises.

A shallow breath is typically breathing into the lungs only. When calm, you should be able to take very slow, shallow breaths without the concentration that accompanies deep breathing. A few general rules about breathing on the cool down exercises:

- Inhale before you begin a stretch.
- Exhale as you stretch.

While stretching, continue a natural breath. *Don't ever hold your breath.*

STRETCHING

Seated Hamstring Stretch

This exercise targets the hamstring, the muscle at the back of your thigh, as well as your back.

STEP 1: Sit on the floor with your legs stretched straight out in front of you and your feet in a flexed position with your toes pointing toward the ceiling (figure 9.1, step 1 on page 126). Always start with good posture, so make sure that your back is straight and your chest is out. Extend your arms over your head with your shoulders relaxed and down. *Inhale.*

STEP 2: As you *exhale slowly*, bend forward and reach for your toes (figure 9.1, step 2 on page 126). The ideal position is to keep your back flat as you hold on to your toes with relaxed arms and shoulders. Few people actually stretch comfortably this far, so stretch only as far as is comfortable for you. If you can only reach as far as your shins or your knees, only go that far. It is more important that you keep your posture—straight back and straight legs—and get the feeling of the stretch while staying relaxed.

Hold for ten seconds with shallow breathing throughout.

9.1 SEATED HAMSTRING STRETCH STEP 1

STEP 2

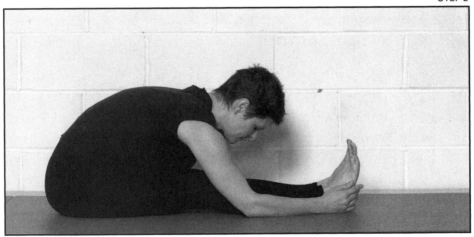

STEP 3: Slowly come back up to sitting posture while *inhaling*. Take a couple of slow breaths before repeating two more times.

Seated Hamstring Stretch With Legs In

If your legs are so tight that you cannot get low enough to feel this stretch in your back, start out with your knees bent and your feet flat on the floor as close to your bottom as possible. Reach around your knees and hold onto your toes while you gently pull yourself forward over your legs. You should feel a stretch in your lower back.

9.2 SEATED HAMSTRING STRETCH WITH LEGS IN

Butterfly Stretch

This exercise is targeted to loosen up the hip flexors, which are the muscles on the sides of your hips.

STEP 1: Sit on the floor with your knees bent and the *soles* of your feet together as close to your body as you can (figure 9.3, step 1 on page 128). Your knees will drop out to the side like butterfly wings. Hold onto your

ankles with both hands. Keep a nice straight posture with your back straight and your chest up. Once in position, *inhale*.

STEP 2: By gently pressing your elbows onto your knees or thighs, *exhale* and relax your knees toward the floor.

STEP 3: Once your knees are either on the floor or as close as you can comfortably get, *inhale* and then *exhale* as you bend forward over your legs, bringing your chest toward the floor with a straight back. It is more important to keep the posture of a straight back than it is to reach the floor; *don't hunch your back* in an effort to get down. It is about stretch and direction of movement, not about touching the floor.

STEP 4: Hold in this position for ten seconds. Remember to breathe normally; don't hold your breath. Each time you *exhale* try to relax your body even more. Don't try to stretch outside your comfort zone as this will cause your muscles to tighten instead of loosen. Over time you will develop greater flexibility.

STEP 5: Return to an upright position, take a relaxed breath, and repeat two more times.

Straddle Stretch

This stretch is for the lower back, inner and outer thighs, and the hamstrings.

STEP 1: Sit with your back straight and legs spread out wide in front of you as far as is comfortable. Keep your legs straight with no bending at the knee and your feet flexed so that your toes point at the ceiling. To keep your feet flexed and knees straight, you will feel that your thigh muscles are taut. *Inhale* as you raise your arms above your head so that your elbows are next to your ears.

9.4 SADDLE STRETCH   STEP 1

STEP 2: *Exhale* as you reach both arms down over your left leg and reach for your toes (figure 9.4, step 2 on page 130). Reaching with both hands will give you a better stretch. Again, the object is to get your maximum

comfortable stretch. If you cannot reach your toes without bending your knees, rest your hands on your shins, knees, or thighs. Feel the bend from your tailbone and keep your back straight from there all the way up to your neck; *do not* hunch your back over.

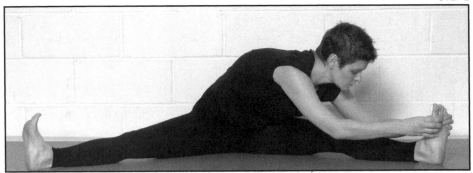

STEP 3: Hold over your left leg for a count of ten while breathing gently.

STEP 4: Move your arms and your body to the middle of your legs without coming up. Reach your hands out in front of you and hold for a count of ten. Don't forget to keep breathing and relax into the stretch with each exhale.

STEP 5: Staying low, reach your hands toward your right foot and hold again for a count of ten. Raise your body up as you return to the starting position. You may wish to bring your legs straight in front of you and gently shake them a little when you are finished with this stretch.

Cobra Stretch Into Child's Pose

This stretch is taken from traditional yoga. We've just done a lot of forward bending, so it is important that we even out the stretch and do a backward bend.

STEP 1: Lie on the floor face down in a pushup position with your palms flat on the floor next to your chest. Keep your legs straight with your toes relaxed inward and your heels relaxed to the outside. *Inhale*.

9.5 COBRA STRETCH INTO CHILD'S POSE STEP 1

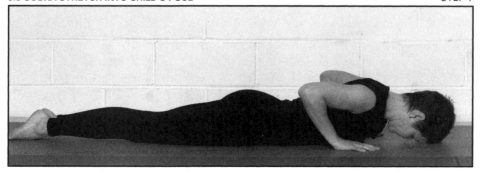

STEP 2: As you *exhale*, raise your head and chest off the floor. *Keep your hips in contact with the floor*; do not raise your chest so high that your hips leave the ground. As you push up with your arms, feel as if you are drawing a line from the floor to the ceiling with your chin. In the final position, your elbows will be slightly bent, not stiff, and your gaze will be towards the ceiling.

STEP 2

STEP 3: Breathe softly as you hold for a count of ten.

STEP 4: As you *exhale*, slowly lower your body back to the floor starting with your chest, then your neck, and finally your head.

STEP 5: Push your body back so that you are sitting on top of your bent legs with your arms stretched out on the floor in front of you and your forehead on the floor. If you have difficulty sitting on your legs, spread your knees apart but try to keep your feet together. You should feel a nice stretch in your upper and lower back and shoulders. You can increase this stretch by crawling forward with your fingertips. Hold for a count of ten before raising yourself into a seated position.

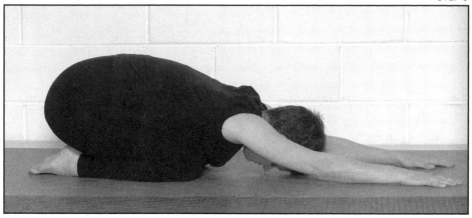

Upper Body and Arm Stretch

STEP 1: Stand with your feet a little more than hip width apart with your arms at your sides. *Inhale.*

9.6 UPPER BODY AND ARM STRETCH   STEP 1

STEP 2: *Exhale* as you bend your torso at the waist to your right side while your left arm extends over your head (figure 9.6, step 2 on page 134). Your right hand can rest on the side of your right leg. The secret to making this a great stretch is twofold. First, keep your chest fully facing the wall in front of you; don't cave in or face downward. Second, imagine trying to touch the wall to the side of you with the out-

stretched fingers of your reaching arm while keeping it directly over your ear. Hold this position while breathing for a count of ten.

STEP 3: *Inhale* as you raise yourself back up to standing position. Repeat the stretch to the opposite side.

✳✳✳

By completing one of each of these stretches in the cool down, you perform enormous benefit to your mind and body. Many people, including professional athletes, overlook this part of the workout either because it is not part of a traditional workout session or because it is not as intense, and so it does not feel as important as the traditional exercises and drills. However, it has become widely recognized that increased flexibility can prevent injury and improve performance, and that visualization can be a key to confidence and success. So discipline yourself to include the cool down in your workout and training sessions.

CHAPTER TEN

THE ULTIMATE BOXING WORKOUT

This chapter is to help you design your workout so that you can accomplish your goals, whether they are to simply get physically fit or to get into shape for the ring. A general rule for working out is quality over quantity. You will benefit more by doing the exercises correctly and doing less than by exercising with poor form, which does not work the muscles as well and can lead to injury.

Your ideal workout schedule is about one hour to one hour and fifteen minutes, five times each week. It is not necessary or advisable to work out every single day. Even professional athletes take days off to rest and rejuvenate the body.

As a boxer, also add running to the workout schedule. Running is done at a separate time from the actual workout because you will not have the strength in your legs to get the full benefit of each workout if done together. Usually running is done in the morning and the workout is done later in the day. While running is necessary training for stamina in the ring (and we'll review how to make running specific for the sport of boxing), you may choose to add it to your workout or not. Many people enjoy boxing as a workout but don't run because of time constraints or other reasons. Whether you add running to your workout or not will depend on your personal goals and preferences.

The only consistent set of exercises that you will do every time you work out are the dynamic stretching for the warm-up (see chapter five) and the cool down exercises (see chapter nine). These exercises should take about five minutes apiece, totaling ten minutes of your workout time. The exercises laid out in these chapters are geared to prepare and repair your entire body, so don't skip them.

The remainder of your workout is more flexible; pick a few of the exercises from each section of the sample workout planner on pages 142 and 143 and focus on those. For example, as a beginner, pick some of the basic exercises as part of your workout, and as you advance select more challenging variations. With the jump rope part of the warm-up, don't do the same exercises every day; mix it up. Once you are proficient with the rope, do freestyle rounds where you change from one movement to another within each set. In the bag work part of the "Training and Conditioning" section, you may want to focus on your jabs one day and on slipping the next. Use the workout planner as a guide for the overall structure of the session and refer to the personal workout scheduler starting on page 160 to select the exercises that meet your individual skill level.

MUSIC

Music is used in most workouts because it is enjoyable and motivating. In boxing it can also enhance your workout by helping you get rhythm in your punches and footwork. Techno music has a fast beat that stimulates brain impulses, which makes the body move at a faster pace. I like to listen to rap to get in a fighting mindset for shadow boxing and bag work. It is really a personal preference, but whatever you choose, find something with a strong, fast beat and get the music cranking. For the cool down period, change the music to a slower style to put you in a relaxed frame of mind.

RUNNING

Running is part of a boxer's training because it builds endurance. In order to develop the stamina you'll need to call upon in the rigors of a match, you have to practice two types of running. *Interval* running is repetitions of sprints with a one-minute break between them, which mimics the specific timing and movements that you will use in the ring. For example, if a match consists of three two-minute rounds with a one-minute rest between rounds, an interval run training for that match would have you run for two minutes, then take a one-minute rest. This type of running builds the endurance by stimulating the slow-twitch fibers (STF) that we discussed in chapter eight.

The other type of running is *non-interval*. This is a sequence of sets composed of short-distance drills that focus on the fast-twitch fibers (FTF) in your muscles to work on speed and agility, while simultaneously conditioning the body for the time components in a match. The two-minute breaks between sets are an ideal time to add shadow boxing and work on boxing technique.

You will fight three rounds in a boxing match, but in both the interval and non-interval running training you will do four sets. The addition of an extra set is deliberate; training for one more set than you will fight helps to build up stamina and ensure that you will have "something left in the tank" during a match.

Interval running is a high-intensity workout, so it should be done only two times per week. Never do interval running on two consecutive days because you need to give your body time to recover. You should also never run, whether interval or non-interval running, on days when you are sparring or in a boxing match. Fresh legs are important in the ring, and if you run on those days, your legs will tire too quickly.

Before we get into the specifics of the interval and non-interval running, let's review some basics of good running form.

- Always run on your toes; your heels should never touch the ground.

- There should be a spring to your running step.

- Stay tall and hold your body up; don't slouch or let your body cave in.

- Swing your hands and arms forward and back but never across the body.

- When sprinting, your palms should be open and flat, facing each other.

- For non-interval running, have your arms and hands in the boxing stance (lightly fisted and in front of your body with your elbows close to your sides).

- Keep your head and shoulders relaxed and your jaw slightly open. The rest of the body takes its cues from the head. If your head and shoulders are tense, the rest of your body will be as well. Your system can produce up to ten times as much lactic acid through tension, which will increase fatigue and soreness.

- Breathe in through your nose and out through your mouth.

Interval Running

The sequence for interval running is a one mile warm-up run followed by a few minutes of stretching the body before beginning the 600-meter sequence sprints. Each 600-meter sprint should take about two minutes to run, thereby imitating a two-minute boxing round.

Warm-up: Run one-mile at 65 percent intensity.

Cool down: Do the five-minute cool down session for stretching and flexibility.

Interval running: Run at 75 percent (run hard), with your hands open, palms flat and facing each other.

SET 1: Do four 600-meter runs with a one-minute cool down between each. After the last 600-meter run do the five-minute cool down again.

SET 2: Repeat.

10.1 INTERVAL RUNNING

Non-Interval Running

The sequence for non-interval running is a one-mile warm-up run followed by sets of jogging in forward, backward and side-to-side motions, with breaks of shadow boxing in between. Once a week, add a long-distance run of two or three miles to the end of the non-interval sequence.

Warm-up: Run one-mile at 65 percent intensity.

Sequence running: Run at 65 percent intensity, keeping your hands up in boxing position.

SET 1
- 200-meter jog
- 100-meter backward jog
- 50-meter side shuffle left
- 50-meter side shuffle right
- Shadow box for two minutes

SET 2
- 400-meter jog
- 100-meter backward jog
- 50-meter side shuffle left
- 50-meter side shuffle right
- Shadow box for two minutes

SET 3
- 300-meter jog
- 100-meter backward jog
- 50-meter side shuffle left
- 50-meter side shuffle right
- Shadow box for two minutes

10.2 NON-INTERVAL RUNNING

SET 4

- 200-meter jog *with punches* (keep your hands up and add alternating punches left and right as you run)
- 100-meter backward jog *with punches*
- 50-meter side shuffle left
- 50-meter side shuffle right
- Shadow box for two minutes
- Long-distance run of 2–3 miles (once per week only)

WORKOUT SCHEDULE

The sample schedule on pages 142 and 143 should help to get you thinking about how to best plan your own workout schedule.

Use the blank schedule in the appendix to help chart which exercises you do on which day. You should do all of the exercises in the warm-up and cool down sections. Where indicated by (pick 3), select three exercises from that section to work on Day 1 and a different three exercises on Day 2. Photocopy the blank schedule and fill it out to help you keep track of which exercises you worked on each day.

Remember: The goal is to mix it up as much as possible so that you are not doing the same exercises or same groups of exercises two days in a row. In the beginning, select the more basic exercises. Once you have mastered the basics, you can also add the advanced exercises and the variations to your daily selections.

SAMPLE WORKOUT PLANNER

	DAY 1	DAY 2
Running	Non-interval	Interval
Warm-Up	5 minutes stretch	5 minutes stretch
	3 rounds jump rope	3 rounds jump rope
	3 rounds shadow boxing	3 rounds shadow boxing
Training and Conditioning	3 rounds heavy bag	3 rounds heavy bag
	3 rounds double end bag	3 rounds double end bag
	3 rounds speed bag	3 rounds speed bag
	Core conditioning	Lower body conditioning
Cool Down	5 minute cool down	5 minute cool down

DAY 3	DAY 4	DAY 5
Non-interval	Interval	Non-interval with 2-3 mile distance run*
5 minutes stretch	5 minutes stretch	5 minutes stretch
3 rounds jump rope	3 rounds jump rope	3 rounds jump rope
3 rounds shadow boxing	3 rounds shadow boxing	3 rounds shadow boxing
3 rounds heavy bag	3 rounds heavy bag	3 rounds heavy bag
3 rounds double end bag	3 rounds double end bag	3 rounds double end bag
3 rounds speed bag	3 rounds speed bag	3 rounds speed bag
Core conditioning	Upper body conditioning	Core conditioning
5 minute cool down	5 minute cool down	5 minute cool down

* The distance run should be only once a week but may be added to any of the non-interval running days that you wish.

CHAPTER ELEVEN

GETTING INTO THE RING

Making the move from boxing workout to boxing against an opponent involves finding the right gym and trainer to take your skills to the next level. In this chapter we'll review how to find them, what to expect from them, and some basics on learning how to spar and do mitt work. When you take your training up to fight level, you will have extra nutritional needs, so we'll also take a look at how to fuel your body properly.

FINDING A GYM AND TRAINER

Finding the right fit for you will depend on what your personal goals and ambitions are. It is important that you find a trainer who understands what you really want to do and supports you in that goal. If a trainer is not on the same page as you, you may find yourself being pushed too quickly in a direction that you are not comfortable with or that you are not getting the fight action that you desire. To help you understand your goals, let's review some of the different levels of fighting.

For your own safety, you need supervision to pursue any kind of fighting in the ring. Even if your goal is simply to get in the ring to spar for fun or to use sparring as part of your workout to get in shape, you need to work with a trainer.

White collar amateur boxing gets its name from the weekend-warrior types who step into the ring. These bouts are geared for the average person, most of them aged from their late twenties to their forties, who have a regular job during the week. A white collar boxer is not looking for a career in boxing yet wants to experience the thrill of being in the ring. If this is the type of boxing you are looking for, your trainer will insure that you are matched with others in your same weight and experience level. This type of boxing is great to put your skills to the test in a real match, which typically consists of three two-minute rounds. The amount of time or the number of rounds can vary depending on the venue.

Amateur boxing can be more of a career goal with the Olympic Games, the Pan American Games, Golden Gloves, National Golden Gloves, and World Amateur Boxing Championships being the highest level amateur contests. These matches are generally composed of four three-minute rounds but may vary. Amateur bouts are unpaid, so these athletes usually have other employment or go to school.

Regardless, they must work their life around their training and make fighting a priority in order to succeed. Amateurs, unless sponsored by a corporation, are usually responsible for their own expenses, such as travel costs to get to matches, so there is a financial commitment in addition to the physical effort.

In professional boxing, you can find the hard-core "prizefighters" who try to get in as many fights as possible to earn some money. Think Rocky Balboa in the early years begging for his $200 and the date of his next fight. This type of grueling fight schedule cannot be maintained for long, and very rarely does anyone pull a Rocky and get a chance to make it to the big time. However, most professional boxers have had a long amateur career before turning pro. This allows time for them to develop a good foundation of skills as they go through the ranks.

Finding a gym with credibility may take some research. Check the phone book or go online to find local facilities and gather some basic information. Be sure to actually visit any prospective gyms so you can see the facility for yourself and ask questions. Questions you should ask include: Does this gym have a boxing team? Do they currently train amateurs and/or professionals? What kind of reputation do they have? The big-name gyms are often a good place to start. Some gyms are cleaner than others, and while this is not an indication of how good or bad they are, it may factor into your own personal preferences. You also need to be sure that their trainer fees are compatible with your wallet. Training session costs can range from $30 to $150 with the average price in the $50 range, depending on your locale.

Once you have selected a few gyms to look at, it's time to find a trainer at the gym. An experienced fighter will know exactly what to look for in a trainer, but, as a beginner, you should do a trial session with three or four different trainers to get a feel for the different ways they work with you. Don't lock yourself in right away; give yourself some time to look around and try out different trainers. Ask them who they have worked with or what they personally have done in their career, but be aware that this should only aide your decision, not make it. For example, being a great fighter doesn't guarantee that he has the ability to train others well. The opposite is also true. I have worked with amazing trainers that have grown up in the sport, know the art of the sport and truly understand it, but they were not accomplished fighters themselves.

A trainer does more than just offer instruction. In sparring sessions, a good trainer will stop the session if you are getting hurt more than you are learning. He monitors the sparring to maintain clean fighting and not allow emotions to get out of hand.

A trainer should listen to you and your goals. I have trained talented kids that I've felt could really go somewhere, but they really didn't want to compete at a high level for whatever reason. I had to back off and not push them because you have to respect people's personal limits. Trainers should offer motivation and encouragement; they shouldn't push you beyond your own comfort level.

The most important element to look for in a trainer is *trust*. Without it, you stand a good chance of getting hurt. Here are some things that a trainer does to protect you:

As a beginner, you may be assigned to fight opponents that you know nothing about. A trainer knows what to look for in an opponent. He can make sure that you are matched up with someone in your weight class with the same experience level. Sometimes fight organizers will throw a beginner with only a couple fights of experience in against a boxer with thirty fights under his belt because they are in the same weight class. This will be a bad experience for the new fighter and should be avoided. That's where a trainer can help.

Once you have found a trainer who is affordable and trustworthy with a good reputation, and with whom you have a good rapport, let the action begin.

SPARRING

After you develop your offensive and defensive skills and condition your body properly, you can bring your training to another level with sparring. Sparring allows you to apply the skills that you have already learned in a more realistic situation. It can also be used as a learning tool to evaluate

11.1 SPARRING

your strengths and weaknesses, which can help you improve your overall boxing skills and develop as a fighter.

You have to remember that sparring is not a real match! This is easier said than done because the adrenaline can really start to flow. So you need to make sparring as safe as possible.

- First, you must have a partner that has control and will heed the trainer.

- Second, you must have a boxing coach or trainer supervise the sparring session to ensure that the contact between you and your opponent doesn't get out of hand. A coach or trainer can also provide sparring drills that will cater to your specific needs and give suggestions on improving the mechanics of your movements.

- Third, make sure you wear proper sparring gear before you step into the ring. This includes headgear (soft helmet), mouthpiece, and groin protection. Women should wear a chest protector.

Finally, have fun! Sparring tests your skills to see how effective your training has been. It can be an uplifting experience and a great confidence builder.

If you are preparing for a match, sparring is the most important aspect of your training. Nothing else can take the place of realistic fighting. You can expect to be nervous your first time in the ring, but the more you spar, the more you will learn how to control those nerves and relax. Nerves take up *a lot* of energy. You can be in incredible shape, but if you step into that ring with a ton of nervous energy, you will be tired out by the end of the first round.

The goal of sparring is to improve as a boxer. You won't do yourself any good to go into the ring with the mindset of knocking your opponent out. You should always have a specific purpose or goal for your sparring sessions. For example, you may wish to work on your defense, and so your focus in the session might be on slipping punches. Or, your goal could be as simple as wanting to work on your jab. Once you are sparring, it can be hard to control your emotions, but try to stick to the game plan. This is another benefit to having supervised sparring: to help you keep your focus.

When done correctly, sparring can be a very gratifying experience. Nothing feels better than training hard and seeing all your skills come together in the ring. In this section, we will review some sparring drills to do with a partner that will prepare you for a boxing match.

Drill 1: Defensive Sparring

This drill involves your partner throwing punches at you. As a defensive drill, your job is to avoid getting hit by utilizing blocks, slipping, and ducking. You will *not* be throwing any punches in this drill.

Your focus will be on learning to read your opponent's movements and react defensively when he attacks.

Begin with your partner throwing jabs at half speed. Over time you will build up the skill and confidence to pick up the pace, but start slow to get used to using your techniques in real time with a real opponent.

After you feel comfortable defending against the jab, try defending right crosses. Then move on to the left hook and finally the uppercut.

Once you feel confident defending against those individual punches both to the head and the body, your partner can attack you with combinations. Remember your footwork and your proper form. Slow it down as you need to in order to make the proper adjustments.

Part of sparring is getting hit. This drill will help you get used to that feeling as you will not be able to defend *every* punch.

Practice: Two three-minute rounds.

Drill 2: Offensive Sparring

This time, work only on your attacks. You won't have to worry about your sparring partner punching back because he will stay strictly on defense.

Start at half speed throwing jabs, then switch to the right cross, then the left hook, and finally the uppercut, until you are comfortable with throwing and aiming each one. Then build combos starting with the simple jab/right cross. Slowly add on until you work your way up to four- and five-punch combinations.

Offensive sparring is also a good opportunity to work on footwork and to get used to controlling the distance between you and your opponent. Once you have worked up to combinations, try mixing up the distance of your attacks by getting on the inside as well as working on the outside.

Just as you were not able to defend every punch in the defensive drill, neither will your partner be able to deflect or avoid every one of your punches. You will be hitting your sparring partner during this drill, and that sensation is another aspect of fighting that you will have to get used to. *Be a good partner and watch the contact.* This means that you should keep good control throughout the drill and don't get overly aggressive. Do not hit your partner harder than you would want him to hit you.

Practice: Two three-minute rounds.

Drill 3: Body Sparring

In this drill, work on protecting and attacking the body. By eliminating any type of head contact, you can get a real feel for fighting without the chance of head blows, which inflict more punishment than body blows. It will also help you get comfortable fighting and throwing punches while in close to an opponent.

In this drill, your sparring partner will attack as well, so you must use both defensive and offensive moves. You can pick up the contact level because there won't be any head contact. Be sure to protect your solar plexus and kidneys by keeping your elbows in close to the body.

As with all the drills, start slowly, learn how to take a body blow and then build your way up.

Practice: Two three-minute rounds.

Drill 4: Free Sparring

Put it all together. It is extremely important that this drill is supervised by a professional trainer or coach. This drill will be the closest thing you will get to a real match. Your trainer might have a certain strategy that he will direct you to work on.

During free sparring it is easy to let your emotions get the best of you. Remember to stay composed and to keep control.

Start this drill at half speed and make sure the contact is in a controlled manner. Don't forget to keep good technique; try not to get sloppy or develop bad habits, such as keeping your hands down or telegraphing your punches.

Practice: Two three-minute rounds.

***

Every fighter has his own rhythm; through sparring, you'll become more comfortable as you start to find your own. You may hear people say that a boxer has "found his rhythm" or is "in the zone," and that is what you need to achieve. Practicing sparring will help you reach that goal by allowing the technique to become second nature.

Through sparring you will also start to recognize others' styles and then utilize that to your advantage. In chapter three on punching, we mentioned how physical attributes contribute to a boxer's individual style. There are many types of fighters with different styles. Since bouts are matched up by weight only, height is an important variable. Not everyone fights the same way, so it is important to identify what type of fighter you are and to recognize an opponent's style. Depending on your body type and skills, you might fall into one of the following fighting categories.

- **Inside fighter:** Usually on the shorter side, the inside fighter prefers fighting close because his arms are not as long and cannot outreach his opponent on the straight punches. A lower center of gravity and close proximity to the opponent's mid-section provides power to this fighter's uppercuts and hooks. Excellent ducking and slipping skills are required for an inside fighter because he'll have to avoid getting hit while working his way to the inside. Jake LaMotta personifies this type of fighter.

- **Outside fighter:** With height comes reach, so this type of fighter is generally tall and long-limbed. He more frequently utilizes the straight punches such as the jab and the right cross, and is a master at controlling distance. To keep his opponent from getting too close, this fighter must have excellent footwork skills both side to side and forward and back. Muhammad Ali is an example of an outside fighter.

- **Brawler:** Usually a stockier body type that prefers to fight on the inside, this tough fighter is known for having a good chin, meaning he can withstand a lot of punches. He is also called a "slugger" because he can throw a very heavy punch. This fighter does not have as much skill or fight as strategically as the inside fighter because he typically throws one punch at a time instead of a combination and frequently leaves himself open for a counterattack. But if you make a mistake and let a brawler land a punch, you will hit the canvas. Rocky Marciano, a four-year heavyweight champion titleholder in the 1950s who has the distinction of being the only boxing champion to retire undefeated, was considered a brawler.

These examples, of course, are generalizations. You will certainly encounter hybrid fighters, those whose skills and ability allow them to effectively work the distance as well as being powerful in close. If you spar multiple times with the same partner, you will start to be able to read him. You'll know what type of punch he might throw next and the timing of that punch because you will understand his rhythm and strengths.

MITT WORK

Mitts are a cross between a boxing glove and a baseball glove. They are sometimes called focus mitts because they help train your body to react quickly as if by second nature. Your trainer wears the focus mitts and throws them up in different patterns while you try to connect with a variety of punches. Like in sparring, you are trying to hit a moving target. Unlike in shadow boxing, you create impact that helps build endurance and "real feel" skills. And unlike with bag work, where you may get sloppy because you are working alone and need to self-correct and self-motivate, here you have a trainer pushing you to keep good form, sharpen up your punches, correct errors, and take it up a notch. During your search for a trainer, you may find that each one has his own special twist to his instructions, such as adjustments to the foot positioning in your stance or how straight or bent to keep your knees. So expect that techniques will vary

11.2 MITT WORK

from trainer to trainer. You can also work with a training partner, a boxer that you trust, where you help each other on drills.

Here are some basic drills that you can expect to do with a trainer or a training partner. Do three rounds of each drill, each lasting two to three minutes.

Drill 1: Combination Punches

Do the standard combination punches that were covered in chapter six. You may work on a specific combination or multiple combinations.

Drill 2: Defense and Counterpunches

The trainer attacks you with the focus mitts so that you can practice blocking. Warning: You will get hit sometimes, and some trainers will hit you repeatedly as a way to help train you to react quickly.

Drill 3: Free Round Drill

Work on different punch combinations. This drill can be really challenging as each punch combination is usually given a number (for example, 1 = jab, 2 = jab/cross, 3 = jab/cross/left hook). Sometimes you will need to memorize as many as eighteen different combinations, but eight to ten are what most people can handle. Your trainer calls out the number, and you throw that combination. This takes physical as well as mental focus and skill.

NUTRITION

When training for the ring, you may need to adjust your diet. Depending on what weight class you wish to compete in, you may need to gain or lose a few pounds as well. In this section are some suggestions on how to do this in a healthy way.

Smart training needs to work together with eating right and using nutritional supplements when necessary in order to achieve and maintain a great body. All bodies require the six basic nutrients: carbohydrates, fats, proteins, vitamins, minerals, and water. Boxers need to balance these nutrients in a special way to provide both the energy and stamina required during a work-out, sparring session, or fight and to aid the body in healing afterward.

Athletes seem to do best when following a 60 percent carbohydrate, 15 percent protein, and approximately 25 percent fat meal plan. If you are trying to lose weight, you need to lower the carbohydrate and fat percent-ages and raise the protein while also increasing fiber.

Carbohydrates

A boxer's daily intake should be 55–60 percent from this nutrient group. Look for foods that are complex carbohydrates that have a low glycemic in-dex. This means that when these foods are broken down to simple sugars in the body, they will not affect the body's sugar level as much as a food with a high glycemic index. Spikes in your blood sugar will not provide the sustain-able energy to muscles that will keep you going. A "sugar rush" will provide an initial boost but will quickly lead to an energy crash. The low sugar carbo-hydrates will keep muscles fully functioning longer and keep your brain alert.

Good foods to look for are whole grain pastas and breads, potatoes, fruit, and legumes. Try to avoid foods that are highly processed, such as white bread, rice, and cakes, or anything fried.

Fats

Fat has become a bad word, as many people have acquired too much of it; however, it is essential to the body's proper balance and should make up 20–25 percent of your diet. Without a certain amount of fat, the body perceives starvation and will start to use up muscle. Fat is also a key to your body's hormone production, and testosterone cannot be formed without it.

A great way to get your requirement of fats is through omega oil (fish oil) supplement. If you eat fish, salmon has the highest concentration of this nutrient. Most people should take four to six grams per day; a hard-working athlete can take up to ten grams. Another fat, peanut butter, is also a protein so it can be a beneficial part of your diet. If you are looking to maintain or add weight, add peanut butter to a meal. If you need to lose weight, use smaller quantities of peanut butter along with apples or celery as a healthy replacement of a larger meal.

Protein

This nutrient is important because it is absorbed very quickly and works to restore, regenerate, and repair the muscles that are broken down. It should comprise about 15–20 percent of your daily intake.

We recommend that you eat protein snacks such as beans, nuts, fish, poultry, eggs, or milk throughout the day. Women can also add soy. This is not recommended for men as it can raise estrogen levels.

Whey protein, a fast-acting protein, is great for both before a training session to prepare your muscles and after to restore them.

Use this as a good guide to your own protein requirements based on your individual weight and activity levels. Multiply your body weight (in pounds) by the grams listed in the chart for your activity level.

For example, a 150-pound individual who is sedentary (works out zero or one times per week) requires 60 grams of protein: 150 x 0.4 = 60.

WORKOUTS/WEEK	ACTIVITY LEVEL	GRAMS OF PROTEIN
0–1	Sedentary	0.4g
2–3	Active	0.4–0.6g
3–5	Growing (youth)	0.6–0.9g
4–6	Building	0.6–0.9g
4–6	Fat loss	0.8–1.2g

Vitamins

The basic vitamins, A, B, C, D, E, and K, are required in more elevated levels for the strenuous work of boxing training and fighting. They can easily be obtained through multivitamins and supplements. It is important to listen to your body and pay attention to how you feel and adjust accordingly. A prime indicator of how your body is balanced is your urine. It should be a pale, lemonade color. If it too colorful or dark, then it is likely that you either have too much of a particular vitamin or you are not drinking enough water. Start by drinking more water. If your urine is still dark, try reducing one vitamin at a time to see if it makes a difference. Always check the recommended daily allowances for your gender and body type on the vitamin bottles and stay within those levels. Again, your trainer or a nutritionist can be a guide. Remember that even vitamins can be harmful if you overdose on them.

Although vitamins work in complex and numerous ways in the body, a quick review of the importance of each of these for boxing may be helpful. Vitamin A helps to protect the skin and tissues both inside and outside the body. The B vitamins are involved with energy production through metabolic functions and will help you feel less tired. Vitamin C produces collagen, which is the strengthener for muscles, blood vessels, and other parts of the body. Vitamin D works synergistically with calcium in maintaining strong bones. Vitamin E is integral in maintaining and protecting the intracellular membranes and will help your skin endure the rigors of the sport. Vitamin K is potassium, and although it is needed in relatively small amounts, it is important in blood clotting and bone metabolism. For boxing, it is essential in reducing muscle spasms and leg cramps.

Minerals

While important to overall health, dietary mineral intake will not make or break an athlete. Eating healthy meals consisting of whole grains, fruit, green vegetables, beans, and nuts is always recommended to ensure proper mineral intake. For intense training, taking multivitamins with mineral supplements is ideal.

Water

Since 60–65 percent of your muscles are water and 6–8 pounds can be lost in a single workout, you obviously need to drink lots of water to prevent dehydration. A boxer in competition should drink 8 ounces of water every waking hour up to 1 gallon a day. If you are doing a boxing workout or training, your intake should be about half that, or 4 ounces each hour up to a ½ gallon a day. You need to keep drinking water all day, not just while you are training, because water can combat soreness by flushing out lactic acid, a byproduct of the stress your muscles undergo during a workout.

There are many benefits to drinking a lot of water. Being well hydrated reduces muscle cramps and muscle pulls and reduces the risk of injury because the muscles work better when their cells are full. But, *drink before you are thirsty; don't wait.* Thirst is a side effect of dehydration, so if you are feeling thirsty you are already somewhat dry.

Water is good to cool you down during a workout, but ice water may shock the system. It is best to drink water at room temperature or slightly cool.

Sample Menu

As discussed, nutritional needs vary depending on many factors, including size, optimal weight goals, energy expenditure, and body composition. Your menu will vary accordingly.

Provided here is a sample menu for a twenty-seven-year-old male boxer, who is 6'2" tall and weighs 198 pounds. The menu plans for energy expenditure of training twice a day for a boxing event of three two-minute rounds, which would mean a total fight time of nine to fourteen minutes including rest.

This menu is only provided to give you an idea of a fighter's diet. You will need to work with your trainer or nutritionist to develop a personalized menu that matches your characteristics and goals.

BREAKFAST

- ½ grapefruit
- ¼ cup maple syrup
- 4 medium pancakes
- 2½ tsp. butter
- 1 scrambled egg
- 12 oz. 1% milk

MORNING SNACK (DURING EXERCISE TRAINING SESSION)

- 12 oz. sports drink (6% carbohydrate)

LUNCH

- 1 meatball sub sandwich
- 16 oz. non-cola soda
- 1 oz. potato chips
- 1 apple

AFTERNOON SNACK (DURING EXERCISE TRAINING SESSION)

- 12 oz. sports drink (6% carbohydrate)

AFTERNOON SNACK (AFTER EXERCISE TRAINING SESSION)

- 16 oz. orange juice
- 1 banana
- 2 fruit newtons

DINNER

- 12 oz. fruit juice (orange, cranberry, grape, grapefruit, strawberry, etc.)
- 3 oz. whole wheat pasta
- ½ cup pasta sauce
- 1 cup black bean soup
- 2 beef burritos, or 6–8 oz. lean beef
- 1 cup brown rice or baked potato
- ½ pint low-fat ice cream or frozen yogurt

EVENING SNACK

- 1 sandwich: 2 slices bread, 3 oz. boiled ham or turkey, 2 tsp. mustard
- 1 cup 1% milk
- 3 sugar cookies

NUTRITION ANALYSIS

- 5,075 calories for two workouts a day (use half this amount for one workout a day)

NUTRIENT	% OF TOTAL CALORIES
760g carbohydrate	60%
160g protein	13%
155g fat	27%

This menu meets this athlete's needs for total energy, carbohydrate, protein, and fat, and exceeds his Recommended Dietary Allowance (RDA) for vitamins and minerals.

Maintaining consistency in your boxing workouts and eating habits will provide you with a fit, well-toned body that will help you to live your life with increased confidence and higher energy levels. *Train hard and eat right*. Repeat this formula each day for great fitness and success whether you are in or out of the ring.

PREPARING FOR THE RING

After working with a trainer, you may wish to get in the ring for real. To do that you need to adjust your training. Taper down your training the week before an event so that your body is not tired. Keep your warm-up and cool down periods the same and adjust the conditioning, boxing and running portions of the workout. If your fight is on Saturday, the tapering down might look like this:

- **Monday:** Warm-up, conditioning and boxing at 75%, cool down

- **Tuesday:** Warm-up, conditioning and boxing at 50%, cool down

- **Wednesday:** Warm-up, boxing at 25%, cool down

- **Thursday:** Warm-up, boxing at 15%, cool down

- **Friday:** Shadow box a little, if at all, rest and relax

If you do run, do it Monday or Tuesday. Don't run after that because you want your legs to be fresh.

As you can see from the schedule, conditioning stops mid-week. Focus on the boxing and keeping sharp those two days.

On the day of the fight, here is what to expect. For all fights, but especially your first, expect to be nervous. Being nervous is good because it gets the adrenaline flowing for the fight and keeps you sharp. However, being overly nervous takes a lot of energy because you tend to tense up. Tensed muscles tire quickly and don't respond as well, which can lead to mistakes and a loss of focus in the ring. I recommend that you eat a good breakfast such as oatmeal (carbohydrates for stamina), eggs (protein for strength), and orange juice (for energy). Some people prefer not to eat at all on fight day, but I like to have something in my stomach for the fight.

Once you get to the venue you will be weighed in. If you have been starving yourself to make weight, you may want to grab something to eat now as you will usually have plenty of time before the actual fight. Don't go crazy and eat a lot, even if you feel really hungry, because overeating will make you very sluggish.

At most white collar matches, there will be several divisions fighting on the same day. So, if you are thirty-five years old and in the beginner division and they start with the nine-year-olds, you may go toward the end of the day. This means that after weigh in you will have a long wait ahead of you and a lot of time to get nervous. Here are some suggestions to get you through that time: Walk around and familiarize yourself with the venue. Get comfortable with the atmosphere of the place, locate the bathrooms, and know where to get water and sports drinks. Find a spot where you can have some alone time that has enough space for you to get your body warmed up. But don't warm up just yet.

Many athletes have problems with the wait. It takes experience to learn how to deal with the jitters both mentally and physically. If you get anxious and warm up too early, you can get into a cycle where you cool down and warm up again and cool down and warm up again and then have nothing left for the match. Instead, try to get an approximate fight time and relax until about a half hour before. Since you will never have an exact start time, the trick is to be relaxed, yet ready. People relax in different ways. I like to lie down and listen to soothing music. You may want to read a book or have a friend with you to talk to. Thirty minutes before your expected fight time, do your warm-up exercises. During the warm-up is when I change my music to something more invigorating to get myself mentally ready. You should go into the ring with a light sweat so that your body is ready to go. Don't go in cold; you will be more likely to make mistakes.

Once they are in the ring and the bell goes off, most people find that their nerves go away and they are focused on the fight. Here is where you trust your conditioning and training. Have fun. If you've put in the hard work, you should feel confident to go out and put your skills to the test. Your adrenaline takes you to another level and you won't feel the punches as you may have imagined you would. Proper conditioning is the key in amateur boxing because the busier fighter, the one who throws more punches, is more likely to be the winner. This is because winning is based on points scored from hits more than from getting a knockout. Don't hold back because you think that you need to save energy for the end of the fight. You have trained and conditioned your body to go the full rounds—this is what you have been working toward—so keep up a barrage of punch attacks.

AFTER A MATCH

If you are well prepared and in condition, the match will be over before you know it. If you are not fully conditioned the three minutes can feel like three hours. How you feel will be a good indication of how your training and conditioning regimen works for you. Winning feels great, but you also need to know how to handle not winning.

If you are a weekend warrior and you just wanted to try it once to experience the thrill of the ring, you should feel good whether the final outcome was a win, a loss, or a draw. It takes a lot of hard work and courage to get in the ring, and you should feel proud that you did it. If you feel that you want to continue, then use it as a learning experience for next time.

If you are younger and are looking to establish yourself as a National- or Olympic-level competitor, a win or loss can be a more difficult thing to deal with because there is more on the line. When you lose, try to pinpoint things that you could have done better and learn from your mistakes. Stay positive and focus on the next fight. Don't get caught up in what you did yesterday; it is over and done and cannot be changed. What you can affect is your attitude and your ability to move forward. Winning can also present challenges to the mental state of an athlete. There can be a lot of pressure when you are on the top because you are the one to beat and everyone expects you to win. There is something to be said for being the underdog because you have nothing to lose.

But winner or not, realize what you will gain as a person. You will find out who you really are when you dig deep into yourself for strength and courage, whether to get over the disappointment of losing and continue the hard work of training until the next fight, or facing down the pressure of winning. Always remember, you came here for the thrill of boxing, and now you are living it.

PERSONAL WORKOUT SCHEDULE

	DAY 1	DAY 2
RUNNING		
Interval		
Non–interval		
Long distance (once per week on non-interval days only)		
WARM-UP		
DYNAMIC STRETCHING		
Shoulder rotations		
Knee rotations		
Hip rotations		
Neck rotations		
Toe touch		
Side to side		
Waist twist		
Leg stretch		
JUMP ROPE (PICK 3)		
Standard "bunny hop"		
One leg hop		
Running in place		
Switch stance		
Forward/backward		

DAY 3	DAY 4	DAY 5

	DAY 1	DAY 2
Side to side		
Cross		
Hitch step		
SHADOW BOXING		
BAG WORK		
HEAVY BAG (PICK 3)		
Single punch drills:		
Jab		
Right cross		
Uppercut		
Left hook		
Footwork movement drills:		
Forward and back		
Side to side		
Combination punching drills:		
Jab/right cross		
Jab/right cross/ left hook		
Jab/right cross/left hook/right cross		
Jab/uppercut/ right cross		

DAY 3	DAY 4	DAY 5

	DAY 1	DAY 2
Free round drills:		
DOUBLE END BAG		
Stationary drills:		
Jab		
Jab/right cross		
Jab/right cross/ left hook		
SPEED BAG (PICK ACCORDING TO YOUR LEVEL)		
Beginner:		
Right hand		
Left hand		
Alternating hands		
Advanced:		
Doubles		
Alternating doubles		
Alternating triples		
CONDITIONING		
UPPER BODY (PICK 3)		
Pushup		
Pushup with medicine ball		
Pushup with step		

DAY 3 **DAY 4** **DAY 5**

	DAY 1	DAY 2
Chest pass with medicine ball		
Shoulder press with medicine ball		
Bicep curl with medicine ball		
Bicep curl with chest toss		
Tricep press with medicine ball		
Tricep curl with chest toss		
LOWER BODY (PICK 3)		
Squat		
Squat with medicine ball		
Lunge		
Lunge with medicine ball		
Moving forward lunge		
Moving backward lunge		
CORE EXERCISES (PICK 3)		
Sit-ups		
Trademark boxing sit-up		
Sit-up with medicine ball		

DAY 3	DAY 4	DAY 5

	DAY 1	DAY 2
Squat thrust		
Squat thrust with medicine ball		
Squat thrust with ball bounce		
Side to side with medicine ball		
COOL DOWN		
Seated hamstring stretch		
Butterfly stretch		
Straddle stretch		
Calf stretch		
Quad stretch		
Cobra stretch		
Upper body/arm stretch		

DAY 3   **DAY 4**   **DAY 5**

INDEX